KidLead™

"Growing Great Leaders"

Dr. Alan E. Nelson

With Nancy, Jeff, Josh & Jesse Nelson

ISBN: 1-4392-3815-4
ISBN-13: 9781439238158

Visit www.booksurge.com to order additional copies.

What experts are saying about KidLead

If you care about cultivating leadership qualities in kids, you can't afford to miss this remarkable book by Alan Nelson. Filled with an abundance of practical ideas, this book explains new and creative ways of building competence and character in the next generation.

> – Les Parrott, Ph.D., Founder of RealRelationships.com, author of *3 Seconds*

KidLead is a wise and soulful guide for helping young leaders find their place in the world, that place where one knows how and why "I matter." It teaches us how to nurture purpose and contributions and send our young out into the world with hope and focus. I highly recommend it.

> – Peter Benson, Ph.D., President of Search Institute, www.search-institute.org

Practical. Relevant. Authentic. These words describe the book you have in your hand. Kidlead is a tool you can use and a reference guide you can refer to over and over again as you equip your kids to be leaders. If you think your child might be a leader, this is your handbook to coach them on their journey.

> – Dr. Tim Elmore, President of Growing Leaders.com, author of *Habitudes*

Alan taps the soul and future in this book. The bottom line is that kids can lead, and they need a place to exercise their leadership. KidLead shows that children are capable of next level leadership at a young age. It will assist you in empowering your kids to spread their wings of leadership now so they can soar when they are older.

– Craig Jutilla, President of Empowering Kids, Inc.

*The **Lead**Now training program has been a great addition to our after school programs and has enhanced our students' leadership capacity and ability to work together as a team. We are proud to be able to offer such an effective and meaningful program for our children and families.*

– Laurie Corso, Principal in the Poudre School District, Colorado

I think it is invaluable to begin teaching leadership to kids. That's when we're going to influence them for a lifetime of leading. I've been working with national leaders for years, and I believe that the best time to begin training them is when they are young.

– John Kotter, former Harvard professor and bestselling author of
   Leading Change and *A Sense of Urgency*

Dedication

This book is dedicated to Jeff and Marina DeWit, whose lives reflect both the influence young leaders can bring as well as the belief in growing great leaders. I met Jeff as an early teen and watched him grow into one of the finest young leaders in his field. We're proud to call you friend.

I also dedicate this book to George Barna, a friend who sowed the seed of this venture during my malleable midlife maelstrom, and to all the KidLead Certified Trainers and their Koaches. May you succeed greatly and forever be inspired to leave a legacy of leaders.

Table of Contents

Acknowledgements

Thanks to readers: David Sandys, Nina Lewis, Tiffany Miller, Steve Grant, and Roy Pina, KidLead Certified Trainers whose feedback proves that we can accomplish more together than we can as individuals.

Thanks also to MWatts, an extremely fine editor who made this book more effective.

Foreword

KidLead's training was an awesome experience for me. I got to do fun leadership-related activities and hang out with other young leaders like me. I also got to learn how to be a better leader while I was doing all the exciting projects. KidLead showed me what it takes to be the best leader I can be. The trainers and coaches worked hands-on to make us better leaders. They encouraged me to take action when leadership is needed, simple or not. KidLead has taught me not only how to be a better leader but also how to be a more responsible person. This book explains the principles behind the training. I recommend this book to all adults who want to help kids like me reach their leadership potential.

-Daisy White (age 11)

I've always known that I was a leader, but I wasn't sure how to bring out the traits deep inside of me and put them to good use until KidLead. The best part of the process was how much support the Trainers gave me. Through the KidLead activities and training, I learned more about my leadership abilities and that even though we're just kids, we are still able to contribute a lot to our communities and families. After this experience, I ran for student council at my school, since I felt more confident in being a leader and knew how to use my leadership traits. When I was elected to student council, I had an opportunity to use the training I learned and put it to good use. I love KidLead's training and know you will enjoy this book, as a parent or teacher.

-Bryce Gesick (age 12)

Preface

From My Heart

This is the book I wish my parents had read. One of the motivations driving this project and our work with preteens and teens around the country through KidLead is that as I look back at my life, I believe I never reached my leadership potential. I think that if someone had seen my ability and helped me develop it, I would have been more effective as a leader. So this book and our KidLead training curriculum are motivated, in part, as I've wondered how much of my potential I haven't used. My hope is to invest in others so that when my short spurt on earth has lapsed, there will be hundreds of thousands of more successful leaders, due to their early development.

I'm pretty much a typical, middle-aged, white guy. I walk and play tennis, but I'm not going to set any world records athletically. Yet money down says that I could beat the world's fastest man in a race. No kidding. All I'd need … is a big enough head start.

Imagine giving your child a ten- to twenty-year head start on other leaders. Consider the benefits of a large number of young leaders entering our communities, corporations, and nonprofit organizations with the experience of a middle-aged veteran. Exciting, isn't it?

No single book will transform your youngster into the next Abe Lincoln, Mother Teresa, Martin Luther King Jr., Mahatma Ghandi, Winston Churchill or Billy Graham. But KidLead will show you practical ways for giving youth a head start to become effective, ethical influencers who will impact the world for generations to come.

One final note: While I (Alan) am the driving voice behind this book, my wife, Nancy, has been a significant influence in creating the content. She is one of the most exceptional leaders I know and is a

KidLead Master Trainer, amazingly gifted with children and teens. Plus, we've invited our three sons, Jeff, Josh and Jesse, to add their input pertaining to youth leadership. Nancy and I have done what perhaps no sane parent writing a book should do—we've asked them to share their honest feedback as to what we could have done better in developing their leadership potential, in hopes that you can learn from our lapses.

Introduction

A New Idea for Raising Great Leaders

There are few experiences more enjoyable in life than being well led, participating on a team or in an organization that works together with a shared vision toward a common goal. When each member uses his or her strengths, everyone feels fulfilled. Even defeat is less disappointing when it's a part of a well-led team, just as victory is less satisfying when it is obtained amidst dissension, conflict, and dysfunction. Most of us have experienced both in our lives. We prefer being well led. Unfortunately, most people can recall negative leadership experiences more easily than positive ones.

My appetite for understanding how leadership works has persisted most of my life. After completing a doctorate in leadership from the University of San Diego, collecting over seven hundred books on the subject, and writing half a dozen books and over one hundred articles, I knew at midlife that I wanted to invest the second half of my life developing leaders full-time. But a decade of training and coaching adults had jaded me a bit in terms of how much adults can or will really change.

I remember as a boy, Grandpa Larkin asked me to guard a concrete sidewalk he had just poured. He didn't want neighborhood kids scrawling their names or wandering pets leaving their paw prints permanently. Grandpa told me to stand there until it dried. I took my responsibility seriously, making sure that no one or nothing disturbed the sidewalk as long as it was impressionable.

In a way, people are like that sidewalk. Adults are like dried concrete, but kids are wet cement. I began studying developmental processes, and then for three years, along with a dozen volunteers and over one hundred kids, I prototyped an executive-level, high caliber leadership program that is now called **Lead***Now* and **Lead***Well*. Although I was skeptical at the beginning, what I saw convinced me that kids with the right aptitude can learn and articulate leadership principles and skills much faster than adults. The results were so astounding that at forty-nine, with no paycheck in sight, I left my full-time job with salary and benefits to launch KidLead, a nonprofit, educational organization dedicated solely to raising effective, ethical leaders.

In today's world of change, the clarion call for more effective leaders is constant and resounding. With all the transitions happening in society, demand for competent leaders overshadows supply. The last three decades have produced a seemingly nonstop stream of leadership scandals, from Wall Street to Pennsylvania Avenue to Church Road. Our souls mourn the loss of trust due to leaders who disappointed us with hollow character and shallow competence. MBA programs now include ethics courses, hoping to address this moral malaise, while watchdog groups sniff out more power gone sour. Unfortunately, that's too late. Something else is needed to develop the character and competencies of those who would lead. Is there hope or will cynicism prevail? Instead of waiting for graduate school, a decade after most moral psychologists believe that character has been cast, why not raise a generation of robust leaders by training them how to lead while they are still moldable?

This book is a compilation of our team's work and discoveries. The final chapter describes the training program itself. Our society needs serious leadership training that teaches kids how to be effective, ethical leaders. Most youth programs labeled as "leadership" teach general character development, serving, assertiveness, and self-esteem instead. While these qualities are important for life in general, they do not specifically focus on leading, how individuals influence others to work together toward common goals.

Ten Benefits for Those Who Read This Book

KidLead is a book that shows parents, teachers, coaches, and children's workers how to identify kids with various degrees of influence aptitude, as well as develop them into ethical leaders while they are still malleable. Here are ten ways we believe this book will benefit you and the children you influence.

1. You'll learn to identify leadership aptitude indicators in children, often observable before preschool. These indicators typically emerge during early socializing, so astute adults can discern who may benefit the most from intentional development. You'll be shown how you can obtain a free diagnostic tool called the Social Influence Survey. It will further clarify observable influence aptitude.

2. You'll learn how to recognize behaviors that diminish leadership development. Parents and teachers often wilt the spirit of a leader because of their own overbearing personalities or in trying to gain control and compliance. We'll alert you to common ways adults inadvertently do this so that you can avoid it.

3. You'll learn how to diminish the negative influence of young leaders behaving badly. Most adults do not understand the difference between a young leader trying to explore his or her influence capabilities and typical, childish misbehavior. Leaders not given specific guidance often act out, causing friction in families, classrooms, athletic teams, and neighborhoods. Teachers can significantly reduce classroom disruptions by applying some very simple but counterintuitive tactics.

4. You'll learn practical ways of developing the leadership aptitude in children. As we've interacted with kids and their parents and developed trainers through our KidLead programs, we've uncovered best practices that you can apply with your children. These principles will help you unlock your child's leadership potential, often by tweaking everyday activities.

5. You'll learn why teaching ethics in the context of leadership by the age of fourteen is so important. Moral psychologists believe that most character is in place before the teen years.

Most cultures in history and the world have rites of passage into adulthood between the ages of twelve and fourteen. That leaves us a four-year window when ethical leadership training is most crucial. You'll discover what this window is.

6. <u>You'll learn how to teach your child to distinguish good leaders from bad ones</u>. Kids are drawn to peer influencers. That's why it's essential that they are able to identify positive leadership role models from negative ones, the latter of whom will lead them astray. You can help your child learn how leadership works and how to avoid bad influencers. Everyone, leader or not, can benefit from understanding how it is that individuals influence others to follow them and strive for certain goals.

7. <u>You'll learn key differences between behaving like a parent and behaving like a leadership coach</u>. With a few minor adjustments, you can significantly enhance the decision making ability of your child, the way s/he interacts socially, and his or her emotional intelligence for influencing others. Leadership development is not just a manner of understanding your child; it requires knowing yourself and the way you interact with your young leader.

8. <u>You'll be able to give your kids a competitive advantage for college</u>. More and more universities are looking beyond GPA, and ACT and SAT scores. They look for leadership experience and extracurricular involvement. Military schools actually have a numerical point system for this. By developing leadership skills in your child, you increase the likelihood s/he will find the better college and job. We'll show you how to construct leadership projects to give your child real-world experience that can be placed on a résumé or college application.

9. <u>You'll be able to show your child how to lead up and laterally</u>. Very few books discuss this; most focus on "leading down." Preteens and teens will need to utilize a different approach until adulthood or even middle age. Even then, the changing

style of leading will require upcoming leaders to influence differently than they have in the past.

10. <u>You'll learn a lot about leading</u>. One of the most common things we hear from parents whose children go through *LeadNow* training is how much they learn about leading, themselves. Everyone talks about leadership, but when you break it down into bite-sized chunks, it suddenly makes more sense to a lot of people. We define the essence of leadership and the sixteen most sought after qualities people look for in their leaders.

Plus, we've sprinkled the pages with stories from leadership experts we've interviewed and sometimes their kids. We believe you'll benefit from hearing from some of the best in terms of how they raised their children or how they were developed as young leaders.

Discussion Activators and KidLead Ideas

Throughout the rest of this book, you'll find dozens of designated *KidLead Ideas*. These are practical activities to help you begin applying what you've read. Our goal is to change attitudes and behavior, not just theorize or philosophize.

Plus, we'll conclude every chapter with a few questions designed to help you process the content at a deeper level. These are more effective if you discuss them with your spouse or, better yet, a group of parents, teachers, or youth workers.

Author's Note Regarding the Use of Pronouns

We've tried to interchange the use of male and female pronouns throughout this book. We believe that the ability to lead is not limited by gender, ethnicity, socio-economic status, education, or age.

Section I.

⌘ ⌘ ⌘

Developing Young Leaders:

Strategies

"If you want to change the world,

focus on leaders.

If you want to change leaders,

focus on them when they're young."

-Alan E. Nelson

Chapter 1

Growing a Great Grown-Up

What Leadership Is Not

So you want to grow a great leader? Bravo! The fact that you've begun reading this book shows that you probably understand how important leadership is to the effective functioning of society in general and how leading can open so many doors in life. But we need to begin this book by telling you that leadership is different from success. You can be a success in life and never become a leader.

Success is about reaching our potential. It is about discovering how our Creator made us and who we were designed to be; it is about understanding our innate worth and developing emotional intelligence; it is about valuing people and using our gifts and talents to the best of our ability. This is why we're here on planet earth, to serve others with our gifts so that at the end of our lives, the net impact on the world is in the plus column, not the minus. At the end of the day, the year, the life, it's not about us. It's about others and what we add to society.

So here I am, founder of a national preteen leadership program, telling you in the opening chapter that your child doesn't need to be a leader to be a success. I want to say it up front because over the years we've met a lot of people who are under the impression that if you're not a leader, you don't matter. That's just not true. To be an effective, ethical leader is a wonderful calling in life, but there are many wonderful roles you can fulfill, leader or not.

A lot of us parents, teachers, coaches, and children's program directors hope that our kids will become great leaders. And why shouldn't we? Leaders tend to have more opportunities in life, are better known, and leave their marks on people and the organizations they serve. In addition, leaders tend to receive more perks and higher paychecks, for the most part. Like the old saying goes, "If you're not the lead dog, the view never changes."

Chances are you're reading this book because you want to help someone younger than you achieve more. The older we get, the more we understand that the real hope for the future is in developing our children while they're pliable. If you're around fifty like me, you're in a life stage psychologists say is characterized by a desire to invest in those younger than us so we can outlive ourselves. Again, we applaud you for picking up this book to see how you can help your child and others become more confident, competent, and influential. Way to go.

KidLead is *not* a book on parenting. It's about leadership development, equipping adults to raise leaders who are effective and ethical. Therefore, this may be the strangest opening chapter you'll ever read in a leadership book. During our work with leaders and their families over the last twenty years, and during our time spent developing the KidLead training programs, we've discovered that a lot of people confuse success and leadership. Your child can be a success in life whether or not s/he ever becomes a leader.

Leadership may be the most overanalyzed and underutilized concept in America during the last few decades. Thousands of books exist on the topic, not to mention scores of training programs, degrees, magazine articles, consultants, and discussions. Try googling the words "leadership" and "leader," and you'll be exhausted by the results.

Years ago, Nancy was hired by John Maxwell as the junior high director of the church that John led near San Diego, California. Every week, more than one hundred junior high schoolers filled the room. One of the students was "Kyle," who consistently disrupted the group. Nearly every week, her staff members had a new Kyle story. For some he was just plain irritating: the way he made noises, called attention to himself, and behaved inappropriately. But when Nancy looked at Kyle, she had a different perspective. Kyle looked like a young version of her boss, John Maxwell, so she tried to imagine what he might become as an adult.

When it was time for Kyle to graduate from junior high, Nancy wrote a letter to him.

Dear Kyle,

I want you to know how proud I am of you. I think that you are very talented and that you will grow up to do great things with your life. I believe in you.

Love,
Nancy Nelson

About ten years later, Nancy was speaking at an event when a woman came up to her. She said, "You probably won't remember me, but I'm Kyle's mother."

"Yes," she said. "I remember Kyle. How is he?"

"He's really doing great," the woman said. "He made it through high school and now college, in part, thanks to you."

"What do you mean?" she asked.

"Well, you know that letter you wrote to him in junior high?" Kyle's mom asked.

"I do," Nancy said.

"Kyle kept it taped to his mirror," his mom said, tears welling up in her eyes. "Sometimes, when he was having a difficult time in school or life in general, he'd take your letter down and read it. He'd highlighted in bright yellow, 'I believe in you.' You made a difference in Kyle's life."

Nancy gave her a big hug. "I'm so glad he's doing well," she told her.

That's what kids need. They need parents, teachers, adults, youth workers, coaches, and mentors to come alongside them and speak words of encouragement to them, to see their potential and to bring it out of them, regardless of whether they ever become leaders. Your job is to find what it is that your child is good at so that s/he can excel at it—or at least do better than most. Your responsibility is to fan those flames.

KidLead Idea: Imagine the type of person you'd like your child to become, regardless of his or her leadership ability. Think of 3 people and 2-3 things each you admire about them. Chances are, these are more about who the person is (attitudes, character traits) than what s/he can do or what s/he possesses. Consider how you can foster these qualities in your child.

Reading Your Child

Bestselling author Max Lucado told me some of his ideas on raising young leaders. Max said that one of his favorite quotes is: "'Children are not books to be written, but to be read.' One of the best things we can do for our children is to discover their unique gifts and aptitudes and develop them—not force kids to become what we think they should."

One thing we've noticed in KidLead, as well as during a decade of coaching a variety of our sons' sports teams, is that a lot of us parents have skewed views of our kids. I've talked to numerous volunteer and paid coaches who've told me about the parents of their team, who think their kid is going to be the next MLB, NHL, NBA, or NFL star, even though only a fraction of 1 percent will even make the first cut of pro sports. In fact, only about 3 percent will play their sport beyond high school. There's a difference between desiring the best for our child and thinking s/he is going to become the next All-American, Steven Spielberg, Bill Gates, or President of the United States.

I remember when one of our boys was in T-ball, and a friend and I volunteered to be the coaches. We didn't know a lot about baseball since neither of us played the sport in college or high school. We lived in Scottsdale, Arizona, where there are quite a few professional baseball players. Three of the kids on our team that year belonged to Matt Williams and Kurt Manwaring, who were starters for the San Francisco Giants. The cool thing is that both dads, while being very supportive of their kids, put no pressure on their children or us as coaches. I really appreciated that. Knowing how to encourage those who were less equipped than they were was a sign of good leadership.

Matt and Kurt realized that it was just T-ball. Not always, but usually, high-pressure parents are not the greats but the wannabes, living out their own dreams through their kids. Parents are biased. We should be. But separating a loving bias from a legitimate assessment of abilities and aptitudes is important for the sake of the child.

Sometimes in KidLead, we see parents who have quite different perspectives of their kids than we do. While some of this is normal and perhaps even healthy, it can also become a disservice when we put undue pressure on our children to become what they're not.

> **KidLead Idea:** *Before they see it, you do. Write 5 strengths you observe in your child. After you write them, sit with your child, look him or her in the eyes and tell them your list without disclaimers or modifications. Don't say, "Jill, you can be good with people—not all the time, but if you want to be." Keep it positive. Say, "Jill, you're really good with people! That's a unique ability you have."*

Letting Go of the American Myth

The American culture is a wonderful environment for pursuing our potential. It's a place where people can realize their dreams. But sometimes these values go too far. It's almost un-American to suggest that a person can't become whatever it is s/he wants to be. "Who are you to tell me what I can't be? What right do you have to limit my potential?"

The goal of this book is to unleash leadership potential. An aptitude is a fundamental wiring or orientation that gives us the ability to learn and develop a skill faster and outperform others in a specific area. Positive psychology helps people focus on their strengths. Researchers such as Gallup, Jim Collins, Marcus Buckingham, and others have noticed that people do best in life when they discover and deploy their strengths.

Our goal is not to walk around discouraging people, telling them what they can't do. We are suggesting that parents and those who work with children help them discover their gifts. Every child is filled with incredible potential in a variety of areas. Most parents wouldn't grieve if their child were not a ballerina, a math whiz, a computer geek, a mechanic, or a star athlete. Therefore, if a child is not inclined to lead and shows little interest in influencing others to work together for common goals, that's okay. They may exhibit some of these characteristics later. They may not. Leading isn't for everyone, but if it is for your child, we'll help you develop that potential and begin the development early.

Some people think this kind of talk is elitist, but elitism says, "I'm better than you." Leaders are not better or worse; they're just different. We're looking for those who are different in the social science of influencing, who exhibit an intuitive ability to motivate others to do what they otherwise would not do, especially in groups.

Unfortunately, the typical leader in our culture doesn't begin to receive formal leadership training until the ages of twenty-five through thirty-five, if at all. How sad that kids have to wait so long to not only lead but also to receive skill development in this area.

As a result, we miss a very critical time in the point of young leaders' lives when we can teach them the character components that may make or break their leading as adults. KidLead is about tapping that potential now and developing it so that at the time most leaders begin their formal training, they'll have ten to twenty years of experience. Imagine the difference.

If you watched the early editions of Donald Trump's TV show *The Apprentice*, you saw how intelligent, talented individuals can be incompetent when it comes to leading. Many of these young leaders came on the show, thinking that leading means bossing others and telling them what to do. They frequently failed to organize the team, build camaraderie, and tap the strengths of group members. The reason is that most of these people never received early leadership training. They didn't lack potential, just development. Like most leaders in our culture, the people on the show had not begun learning to lead until they were young adults.

- Leadership is the process of helping people accomplish together, what they could not as individuals.

- Leaders are those who get leadership going.

Defining Leadership

Based on the previous, simple definition, we believe that not everyone can, should, or even desires to become a leader. We realize that this smacks of being un-American and may irritate some reading this book. A lot of people desperately want to believe that anyone can become a leader, but assuming this is a disservice to those lacking sufficient aptitude for learning leadership effectively.

Being a good leader is quite different from being a person of character, confidence, and assertiveness. Having leadership qualities is different from having good self-esteem, caring for others, possessing emotional intelligence, and making good choices. While we want our leaders to have these qualities, you can possess these and not lead. We cannot find any hard research showing that everyone can be a leader, in the organizational sense of the word. If leadership were everything, it would become nothing.

Every child, regardless of leadership capacity, deserves to have good self-esteem, strong character, initiative, confidence, people skills, and a sense of purpose. This is about being a fully engaged, healthy human being, not leadership. The reason we want these qualities in those with leadership aptitude is because a leader's life and decisions affect so many. We all suffer when those who lead us lack these important qualities, as can be seen in the endless string of corporate and organizational scandals. But being a mature person does not make a person a leader.

Denying the idea that everyone can become a leader is not the same as telling someone, "You'll never be a leader." Sometimes, you just don't know if a child has leadership capacity. Late bloomers exist. Family of origin and early childhood experiences can muddy our self-expression. Sometimes, adults shut down the leadership ability in their children, resulting in young leaders remaining incognito. Our goal should be to help those with observable leadership aptitudes discover, develop, and deploy this capacity. Leading, like any other inclination or natural ability, needs to be identified and cultivated. Our responsibility is to assist our kids to be great grown-ups, regardless of their gifts.

Jeff Nelson (the author's son) on the informal influence of leader-parents

I think it helps when you grow up with parents who are leaders themselves. You catch a lot of conversations and experiences that make you feel more comfortable leading yourself. When I was a freshman in college, I started a table tennis club because I like ping pong and there wasn't a club for that at my university. My junior year, I was elected to student government as the student representative that supervised all the campus clubs and student organizations. This opened up other doors to interact with leaders in the university, administration, and around the country. Then I ran for student body president, losing by a few votes. The experience taught me to take advantage of opportunities. Along with my parents' and others' encouragement, I learned to take positive action toward leaving an organization better than I found it.

Three Roles in the Leadership Process

One of the most important things that parents, mentors, and teachers can do in the lives of children and youth is to help them discover their unique signature, which consists of who they are and what they're good at. This empowers them to pursue endeavors they are likely to excel at and enjoy. By this we do not suggest saying, "You're not good at _____" or "You'll never be a _____," but rather identifying where the child's potential lies. Everyone plays one of three vital roles in a typical leadership process. We'll call them the big "L," little "l," and "F."

A big "L" is a person who is a natural leader, someone who will consistently, habitually, and intuitively gravitate toward roles and situations where s/he can express these gifts. S/he feels frustrated in settings where leadership is poor or absent. We estimate that 10-20 percent of people have some degree of this type of wiring. They are what we call "leaders," whether they are leading at the moment or not. These individuals multiply their efforts by organizing others. By investing in these people, you'll likely see significant return because they grasp leadership skills more readily and will influence more people. Focusing on influencers is the forte of our KidLead training programs.

The little "l" refers to a person who can learn various leading skills but does not do it naturally. Exhibiting such actions must therefore be very intentional. Consistent leading wears out an "l," whereas it tends to energize the "L." An "l" can lead situationally but will not likely become a leader as we defined it previously. Sometimes you'll hear adults confess this. "I'm not really a leader, but someone needed to do something, so I got recruited." This person can be a great asset and may find himself or herself in middle management or smaller leadership roles. We estimate that about 60 percent of people are in this range. These individuals who can benefit from training but are far less apt to see the same results as those with big "L" aptitude. Learning to lead is more frustrating, difficult, and less fulfilling for an "l," but it can benefit the leadership process.

The "F" stands for follower. These are very important people, but they shy away from leading and will often run the other direction. We estimate that 20-30 percent of people are strong "F"s. They loathe being put in charge, and others tend to feel the same if they are. "F"s need to understand how leadership works so that they can be healthy, proactive team members and so that they can recognize and avoid bad leaders.

A majority of people are followers most of the time. That's good, since it allows everyone to use his or her talents in areas where they matter most. Leaders help us do that by setting direction and getting us organized. "L"s need to learn how to follow, since leading is not needed all of the time and so they can be more effective at leading. If you have an "L" in your family, you'll want to intentionally develop this quality as well. The world has too many autocratic, self-centered leaders, primarily because these "L"s never learned how to be good followers. But teaching an "F" how leadership works and how to be a responsible team member is quite different from training an "L" how to lead effectively and be a servant.

The bottom line is that "L"s need "F"s, and "F"s need "L"s. Every successful team is made up of "L"s and "F"s.

Since no one can fully predict who will and will not become a leader later in life, our best estimate is to identify those who exhibit observable behaviors and intentionally develop them early. These children are most apt to enjoy and benefit from intentional leadership development, since the best predictor of future behavior is past and present behavior. Whether or not you agree with our concept of leadership aptitude, you'll find ideas for developing your child's potential no matter what his or her capacity.

The graph portrays the approximate percents of "L"s (left side), "I"s (middle section) and "F"s (right side). This is similar to other aptitude curves that depict a small minority with a lot of talent, a majority that has some ability to learn skills through intentional effort, and a trailing minority with low to nil capacity. The goal for those with some ability is to develop it. The others can be educated on how leadership functions so they be positive team players and avoid becoming victims of bad leadership.

Although one might think that those closest to the left axis need not be trained because of their natural ability, the opposite is true. The reason you want to identify and develop these future leaders is so they can get a significant head start on leadership and ethics training, since without the latter they run the risk of doing great damage as they use their influence for bad.

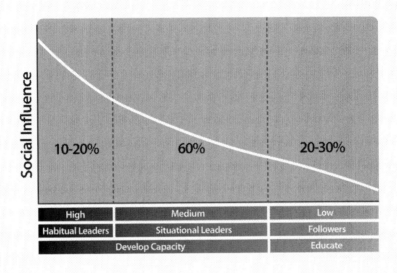

Discussion Activators

1. What is your working definition of leadership? How is it similar or different from the one the author presents?

2. Why do you think it is helpful to distinguish leading from other successful living skills?

3. Discuss this age-old question: Are leaders made or born?

4. Name a few people you know, and practice determining whether they are an "L," "I," or "F."

Children are not books to be written,

but to be read.

Chapter 2

Assess Your Child's Leadership Quotient

I grew up in a farming community in southwest Iowa and attended Orient-Macksburg Elementary School. I remember at recess the kids coming up to me and asking, "What are we going to play today?" Some days I'd pick softball, sometimes soccer, and at other times dodge ball. A couple times after a parent-teacher conference, my folks told me, "Alan, the teacher said you're being too much of a class clown, so you need to settle down." The issue was that as a classroom leader, I was stealing attention away from the teacher, which was disrupting the class. C's in conduct didn't sit well in our house. Looking back, I realize that I was a leader, even though no one ever told me that. Certainly, no one worked to develop me. For me, as for most kids, exhibiting leadership aptitude seemed like more of a negative when it came to adults.

Whether you talk to teachers, coaches, principals, children, or youth workers, you'll hear the same thing: certain kids just seem to have "it." This "it" is the ability to influence others. Well-behaved and self-disciplined ones become allies to adults in charge and usually get rewarded. Those who aren't become pegged as troublemakers, kids who compete with adults and strive to be in charge. Natural leaders influence others around them, whether they try to or not.

IQ (intelligence quotient) doesn't measure wisdom or smarts; it measures a person's capacity for thinking and gaining knowledge, typically in areas such as science, math, language, and critical thinking. There are plenty of people with high IQs who are waiting tables and performing menial tasks. IQ measures a type of aptitude. Genetic testing of pro athletes to identify certain genes is causing some researchers to believe that in the future, a parent will be able to have his children tested to see what type of sports they should pursue if they want to excel. We might think of this as a sort of AQ, athletic quotient.

In his landmark book *Frames of Mind: The Theory of Multiple Intelligences* (1983), Howard Gardner identifies at least eight "intelligences." The problem is that standardized tests and typical schools only focus on two of these, but there are a variety of gifts, aptitudes, and quotients.

LQ (leadership quotient) is similar in that certain people possess an innate ability to learn how to lead faster, easier, and more effectively than others. Ask anyone who oversees groups of people, and they will tell you that a small percentage of individuals exude an inordinate amount of influence. This ability is little different from any number of other aptitudes that measure the likelihood of gaining skills and performing better than the majority. Social science recognizes the role of the catalyst.

Regardless of your philosophy of whether leaders are born or made, what we want to do in this chapter is provide some indicators for what we call early bloomers. These are the kids who are most apt to benefit from intentional training, much the same as a natural athlete, budding math student, or gifted artist. Before our three sons were eighteen, we were the custodians of their bank and stock trade accounts. They could not move money in these accounts without our signature. As with any other resource, parents and teachers are custodians for developing their children's potential.

The following are ten observable indicators that tend to reflect leadership aptitude. These are based on exhibited behaviors we can measure socially. Although having all ten is not required, certainly a strong showing of at least half would seem to imply an inclination toward leading and most likely an aptitude begging to be developed. Granted, some leaders bloom late, but be on the lookout for these characteristics.

Ten Indicators of Leadership Aptitude

1. Peers listen to your child when s/he talks.

Even if everyone is talking, only a few are listened to and taken seriously. Years ago, an investment firm ran an ad campaign stating,

"When E.F. Hutton talks, people listen." Some refer to this as the E.F. Hutton effect. There are talkers and non-talkers, extroverts and introverts. Regardless, leaders tend to be the ones taken more seriously. Don't confuse talkers with influencers. The length of time a person talks is not as important as the weight of what s/he said. Sadly, many kids get overlooked in social settings. While they can benefit from assertiveness training and speaking skills, being comfortable communicating is still different from being heard and heeded. Leaders get their message across no matter how eloquent their public speaking. Watch your child in a social setting and observe how others respond to her while she speaks. Watch others' body language as they respond to your child. How many kids stop what they're doing to hear your child? When standing, how many literally turn their bodies toward your child? These are symptoms of this indicator.

2. Peers seek your child's opinion, asking what s/he wants to do, and then the peers follow.

The difference between indicators #1 and #2 is that if the leader is not present or has not shared his opinion, peers will seek him out to discover what he thinks. Whether it's knowing what to play at recess or getting a perspective on clothing, a video game, movie or song, leaders are sought out by others. People who are "F"s and "I"s do not solidify their opinions until they've gotten input from influencers. The same is true among adults. You can tell the "L"s because you hear their names mentioned in social circles and during staff and board meetings. A few are sought more than most. Children and youth have their own mini-cultures where a minority influences the majority. The difference between social niceties, being polite and listening to others, is that leaders tend to be followed. Others will play soccer if the leader says "soccer" or tag if the leader says "tag."

Leader types are noticed when they are absent or haven't checked in on a subject. "Where's Josh today?" "I haven't seen Michaela." Even in their silence, leaders convey influence. "Jeff, what do you think we should do?" "Angela, do you like it?" Opinion leaders are important in social settings for establishing direction and weighing priorities.

3. Your child initiates projects, seems to have goals/ambitions, challenges the status quo.

Most leader types are not satisfied with long periods of playing video games, watching television, or sitting around. They tend to be active. They get excited about projects. They exhibit a healthy curiosity related to their interests. They neither wait for parents or peers to give them goals nor do they take the path of least resistance.

Sometimes we're asked if this quality is confused with attention deficit disorder (AD/HD). This is the most diagnosed behavior disorder among school-aged children. Around 3-5 percent of children are diagnosed to have this condition. Some experts report that even that number is high. Although I've met several adult leaders who claim to have attention deficit disorder, the big difference between a non-leader with AD/HD and a leader with AD/HD is whether or not others follow. You'll hear this distinction throughout this book because that is the essence of leadership and is what differentiates behaviors done by individuals without influence from behaviors displayed those who lead.

Jeff Nelson, on when he began to see himself as a leader

The first time I began to see myself as a leader was in late junior high. I was musical and asked to be in our youth group band, playing the keyboard and singing. Being on stage and in front of others gave me confidence to be more involved in other areas where my leading could develop. While talent does not make you a leader, a person can use a talent to open doors for leadership that might not happen without the ability.

---

4. Your child has been accused of being bossy, strong-willed, or opinionated.

This attribute can drive teachers, parents, coaches, and siblings batty, but leaders, in general, have more opinions about things than others. Whether right or wrong, they tend to have a lot of thoughts about a lot of things. They are usually willing to share these when asked and sometimes when they're not. A child can be strong-willed and not a leader, but many leaders are strong-willed. Again, the difference often comes down to whether or not others follow.

If your child is not bossy or strong-willed, it doesn't mean that he lacks leadership aptitude. Perhaps he has learned when to give his opinions and is emotionally mature enough to recognize when he should and should not act out, especially when adults are involved. Therefore, an absence of this quality does not necessarily indicate a lack of aptitude, but the presence of this quality often is a sign. This quality stands to benefit from intentional training so that a young leader learns not to offend others and succeeds in *leading up* when adults are in charge. That means influencing superiors and/or people who have more influence.

5. Your child gets selected as class monitor, team captain, or group leader by adults.

I've taught adults that in order to determine who has leadership ability in their organization, they should interview others, listening for influence roles in their past. Adults often spot young leaders in class, religious school, and the ball field, and give them official roles. They frequently do this intuitively to gain the respect of the young influencer and to tap into her natural ability to control her peers. It eases teaching and coaching by decreasing disruptions. Leaving the class under the eye of a student council member or putting the captain in charge of team calisthenics lightens the burden of the adult.

Many leaders' lives hold true to this pattern. Early on, an adult recognized their potential and picked them to run for office, be captain of a team, or manage groups in a company. Those most trusted for direction setting are often selected for roles of influence as youth.

Stephen Covey, bestselling author of The Seven Habits of Highly Successful People, tells KidLead how he helped develop leadership ability in his son, Sean.

One thing that has been significant was to affirm and believe in Sean. When he was in football, we used to have visualization sessions, where he would tell me some of the situations he would face, and then I would get him into a very quiet, meditative state of mind. Then I'd try to describe those situations and try to have him visualize himself responding to a difficult situation or a coach or the huddle or dealing with whatever pressures that would come. Then he would see himself, as clearly as possible, performing at the highest level as possible.

We also used to do a lot of one-on-one dates, where essentially you do things with the kids that they write on their agenda, not yours. You're with them and they know that you care about them. You're not comparing them or doing the activity with a large group. What matters to them also matters to you so that they feel affirmation and unconditional love. The more people who grow up with this type of experience on a consistent basis, the greater the inward sense of security they have that unleashes their own creative potential to make a difference in life. This unleashing of the creative energy is an astounding thing.

6. Your child has been disciplined for being a distraction in class or on a team.

Nancy remembers being singled out and called down by her youth pastor during a church outing. She said, "Everyone's goofing around. Why did you pick on me?"

"Because you're a leader," the pastor responded.

"I don't want to be a leader," she answered.

"It doesn't matter. You are," he explained.

Teaching is hard work, at least teaching well is. Therefore, when a teacher is not skilled in identifying and developing young leaders, s/he often feels competition with a student possessing influence. Later in this book, we have a chapter dedicated to providing teachers with practical ways of developing young leaders in their classroom. But when there's one teacher to fifteen, twenty, or even thirty or more students, compliance is required. If 10 percent of any given class is wired to lead, these students will gain attention naturally. When a budding leader exudes a sense of humor, tells jokes, or makes snide remarks, multiple classmates will transfer their attention away from the teacher or the assignment. The young influencer is deemed a class disrupter and troublemaker.

Non-compliant but non-leader children are far less problematic. They are primarily seen as irritating, but they do not threaten class control. As a result, leaders typically receive more negative attention for inappropriate comments or actions because they pose a greater threat to an adult trying to maintain attention.

7. Your child negotiates well with peers and other adults.

Let's say that your eleven-year old, Jessica, has a bedtime of 9:00 p.m. on school nights, but Jessica is engrossed in a Disney channel movie. "Oh Mom, c'mon. My homework is done, and I'm ready for school tomorrow. Why can't I stay up until ten?"

"Because, honey, you know how rushed it gets in the morning," Mom defends. "Nine is your bedtime."

"But, Mom, this is a really good movie," Jessica responds. "What if I lay out all my clothes, make my lunch, and get everything ready on commercials?"

"I don't know," Mom stammers. "I don't want you groggy in class."

"It's just an hour," Jessica explains. "Besides, I'll help you get sissy ready if you want."

Mom pauses. "Well, okay, but no later than ten."

What happened? Mom was set on having Jessica to bed at nine, but Jessica pleaded a strong case for staying up later. Scenarios like these are quite common among kids with leadership aptitude. They are able to articulate their ideas and present them in such a way that persuades both peers and adults. You'll hear people comment, "Someday, you're going to be a lawyer." They recognize the child's negotiating skills but are also implying that leading is an adult quality, not a young person's.

Jeff Nelson, on the benefit of certain youth activities for leadership confidence

One thing my parents did naturally to teach leadership, perhaps without knowing it, involved sports. Dad coached several years. When you're on a team, planning strategy, dealing with opponents, and playing different roles, you can learn a lot about how leadership works without even calling it that. This carried over into strategic thinking in other areas of my life. In high school, I participated in a youth-in-government program that taught us how the government works and allowed us to actually use the state capitol to pass laws and administrate policies. This also taught me how to get things done in groups where people are vying for their agenda. You have to negotiate to get things accomplished.

---

8. Your child is good at organizing younger children in activities or play.

While adults tend to rely on titles, organizational flow charts, and positional authority, children tend to be more organic in the way they influence. An early sign of leadership aptitude is a child's ability to organize younger children in activities. Perhaps it's getting kids in the neighborhood to play house, or having them take turns on the trampoline, or doling out rules for a game they made up. When you see a pied piper in the neighborhood, chances are, you're observing an emerging leader. Although self-esteem and confidence issues can retard leading among peers and older people, more reticent leaders often display their influencing gifts among younger kids. This often makes them popular babysitters and childcare assistants.

9. Your child stands up for his or her values and is not prone to peer pressure.

This is a good quality come adolescence, when self-centeredness morphs into social awareness and the dreaded peer pressure. Leaders tend to comply less when tempted by others, so long as the temptation goes against their basic beliefs. When moral conscience is missing, even leaders can be persuaded to do things that are unethical, which is one reason why gang members are typically recruited between the ages of eleven and fifteen. Compliant children are more vulnerable to the opinions of others and usually exhibit less leadership aptitude.

The weakness of this quality is that sometimes leaders need to be taught tolerance of others, because they tend to avoid those who do not share their standard of ethics. Their lack of empathy causes them to write off others or avoid them altogether, which is not always what we should do as leaders if we want to be effective.

10. Your child seems to be liked by others.

When we surveyed public school teachers, one of the consistent attributes they noted about classroom leaders was their likeability. Leaders tend to be better groomed, they take care of their looks, and they are generally friendlier than most. This attention to appearance reveals an implicit social skill that leaders understand is important to be effective. While we may avoid the issue of looks, dress, and other externals, research shows that adults exhibit a bias for those who keep up their physical appearance. We tend to vote for taller presidential candidates, identify strength and beauty with influence, and lean toward following those who present themselves well.

Popularity can happen without organizational influence, but most leaders tend to be better liked than others. The wallflower—the loner, introverted, and socially awkward student—is not followed. They can still influence in what they create as inventors, artists, and entrepreneurs, but it is a different influence than leadership. That is why we stress that KidLead training programs are not designed as a charm school or to mainstream the socially challenged. Yet, leaders do need a certain amount of emotional intelligence to be effective, which shows up in how s/he relates to others. Those who are good at relating to others possess the likeability factor.

> **KidLead Idea:** Look at the list of these 10 observable behaviors indicating leadership aptitude. Give your child a rating of 1-4 on each one: 1 non-existent, 2 low, 3 present, 4 strong. How many of the 10 had a 3 or 4? What was your overall sense of evident aptitude, based on this list?

FREE Social Influence Survey

Although a list of ten indicators is a good start, a more thorough assessment can be found in an instrument we've developed for **Lead**Now and **Lead**Well applicants, called the Social Influence Survey (SIS). We named it this because it reveals aptitude by reporting on informal leading behaviors, since most children have typically had few formal experiences as leaders. It is easier for us to look at observable, social influence. The Social Influence Survey also serves as a pre-test and post-test tool for our research on preteen and teen leadership development.

If you'd like a *free* Social Influence Survey for your child, you can go to www.kidlead.com and click on the tab at the top of the home page. There you'll find twenty-five questions with multiple-choice responses. Fill one out on your child. The assessment works even better if you compare it with what others say about your child, so long as they've observed your child in social settings. Parents will receive an automated report with their child's scoring, along with a key on how each question relates to leadership.

Again, this is not a determiner of leadership, but it does strive to reveal aptitude based on past and present social behaviors. To be considered for a KidLead training program, we require two of these to be presented (not more than one from a relative), along with an application for those applying to be a part of a KidLead training program. The reason we require SIS forms is to assess observable aptitude. Those with a certain level of aptitude are invited to participate in a KidLead training program because we've found that leaders learn better from each other. Getting peers with influence together is an important part of our training success.

> **KidLead Idea:** *Fill out a Social Influence Survey for your child and ask a friend, teacher, coach, or neighbor who has seen your child in a social setting to respond to one for your child. Be sure to ask a third party to look at the results or else the other person's answers may be biased for fear that it will affect your relationship with him/her.*

The goal is to figure out as early as possible who has a natural inclination to learn leadership so that we can train them while they are still moldable and give them a significant head start. The stronger the aptitude, the more important it is to take intentional steps to help young leaders reach their potential. The positive psychology movement is teaching us the importance of discovering and developing our strengths instead of spending so much time and energy trying to fortify weaknesses.

Discussion Activators

1. Which of the ten leadership aptitude indicators seemed the most surprising to you?

2. Share a story about you, your child, or a child you know that illustrates one of the leadership aptitude indicators.

3. What are indicators of aptitude in other areas, such as the arts, athletics, crafts, math and verbal skills? Why would leading be similar in terms of a unique set of indicators?

4. Do you agree or disagree with the idea that everyone can learn to be a leader? Why?

We cannot always build the future for our youth,

but we can build the youth for our future.

-Franklin D. Roosevelt

Chapter 3

Five Ways Adults Hinder Young Leaders

Good Intentions, Bad Outcomes

"Watch your step," my dad warned, as we walked down the rows of the newly planted cornfield. "You don't want to crush the new corn." Growing up on a farm, I learned how delicate corn sprouts were. In a few weeks, the stalks would be stout enough to endure windstorms and adult work boots, but sprouts can be easily trampled. The same is true with young leaders.

A friend of mine, who is a respected leader, told me this story.

> The other day I was at a youth sporting event with my dad, watching one of my teenage sons preparing for his game. He was kind of goofing around, having fun as he warmed up, exuding confidence. As I sat beside my father, he asked, "Who's Bradley most like?"
> "He's most like me, Dad," I responded.
> Then my dad startled me when he said, "No he's not. You're quiet."
> I didn't say anything, but I realized at that moment that although I'm a leader at work, whenever I get around my dad, I get very quiet, much the way I did as a child.

The reason is that my friend's dad was a domineering, Type-A person, who demanded compliance and obedience from his kids growing up. Although my friend was indeed a leader as a child, when he expressed his opinions and personal views as a leader-child, they were considered rebellious by his strict, overbearing father. Therefore, my friend became reserved and passive as a boy at home, even though at school and other settings he was outgoing and considered a leader. The father perceived that his son had a quiet, retiring personality, never realizing how he'd snuffed out his son's leadership potential at home.

When I tell this story in my parent and teacher training, nearly every time there are people in the audience who nod their heads. They relate to it because they too experienced the retribution of a parent or significant adult who did not understand their leadership attributes as a child and tried to eradicate them. Whether it is insecurity, ignorance, or any number of other personal issues, many adults hamper the development of budding leaders, causing them to withdraw into emotional caves.

If you confronted the domineering father in the story above, no doubt you'd experience disbelief and remorse that he responded in such a way to stifle his son's leadership abilities. But everyday, scores of young leaders around the world duck into emotional closets in order to survive a world dominated by people who do not understand how to develop a young person with leadership wiring. Like a young bird that gets pecked at for flapping its wings, these leaders become frustrated and confused by the way they're treated by elders.

The purpose of this chapter is to educate adults, not make parents feel guilty. But when we shut down young leaders for expressing their gifts, we set them back. Many late bloomers are merely leaders who've crawled into their shells because significant people in their lives condemned them for what came natural to them. Only after years of maturing and experiencing situations where their leading is rewarded do they become comfortable in their own skin. The following are five of the most common ways that adults shut down the natural expression of youthful leaders as they begin to experiment with their strengths.

Five Ways We Break a Young Leader's Spirit

1. Poor listening and exclusion of their ideas.

You could argue that poor listening skills and an exclusion of ideas would diminish the self-esteem and confidence of any child, but it's even more pronounced with young leaders. Here's why. As we mentioned in the previous chapter, leaders have a lot of opinions and ideas. That is one of their strengths. So when we shut them out of conversations, tell them to be quiet and consistently make decisions without allowing their input, we've pretty much communicated, "Your opinions aren't worth hearing. Your strength is not valued in this family, classroom, or team."

One way we train adults to discern possible peer leaders is to think about people who share opinions with them. Having an opinion does not make you a leader. You may merely be opinionated. But leaders do have a lot of opinions. Their minds are constantly churning, responding internally to people, situations, and possibilities. When non-leaders who are in charge have people around them like this, they often ostracize them as troublemakers, labeling them as negative and critical, but savvy people recognize that these people might be frustrated leaders who want to be heard. They can capitalize on their influence by embracing instead of alienating them.

Ratchet that back a few years and you find children and youth who have a lot of views on various things. Adults fear letting these children air these views because they think that if a young leader expresses an opinion, s/he will take over. Just like adults, though, what children value most is having their voices heard. By allowing people to express their ideas, we help them process their thinking and build consensus, and we also esteem them for thinking. We'll often find, if we're humble, that our budding leaders come up with some really great ideas that will improve whatever it is we're doing. For example, when we were selecting logos for KidLead, we let a group of preteens in one of our **Lead**Now programs select the logo we now use.

Responding to the ideas of young leaders requires emotional intelligence. While we can't always provide ample time and attention for listening, when we consistently quiet our kids, exclude them from adult conversations, and dismiss their ideas as childish because they're young, we telegraph the idea that their natural gifting is not valued. By failing to reinforce their opinions, we communicate that their leadership is not valid. Literally, we're creating leader "invalids."

> **KidLead Idea:** *Watch the movie, Rudy. While this is not specifically about leading, it does portray the common phenomena of a parent who fails to believe in the dreams*

of his son, which tempts to destroy the passion of the child.
Watch <u>Rudy</u> in the context of how adults treat their young
leaders.

2. Treating siblings and peers the same.

Talk to almost any parent with multiple children, and you'll hear
them say, "They're so different from each other." Kevin Lehman is an
expert in the field of birth order. He's the bestselling author of *The
Birth Order Book* and a good book on children leaders titled *The First
Born Advantage.* In his years of research, Lehman has determined that
in addition to personalities and gender, birth order can influence a
child's wiring. Despite parents' acknowledgement that their children
are different, they often try to treat them the same to be fair. If we fail
to distinguish differences and respond to them appropriately, we do
a disservice to our children, even though our intent is to treat them
fairly.

This is true in general and especially when it comes to raising
kids with leadership aptitude. Although we'll deal with this more in
Chapter 5, the point here is that if you try to treat all of your children
the same, you'll fail to develop them according to their potential.
It's similar to an employer reacting to all of his employees alike or a
saleswoman relating to her customers the same way. The most effective
supervisors and service people respond to people as individually as
possible. While you retain the same values for all family members,
you'll want to create unique and effective learning opportunities. This
is but another thing that makes good parenting difficult, because
you need to be adaptable based on what will benefit each child the
most.

For example, in order to help a compliant child learn self-discipline,
the ultimate goal of discipline, sometimes all you need to do is give a
stern look. This modest feedback immediately changes the behavior
of the compliant personality. But if you're trying to raise a leader who
is strong-willed, s/he will not benefit from such a passive approach.
This child needs more assertive, intentional, in-your-face discipline—
that still allows feedback—to register at the same level on his or her
response meter.

For example, children who are nervous typically need more
nurturing and empathy then their risk-taking siblings, who may benefit
more from warnings and guidelines. The goal is to create confidence

in both children, but the methods for accomplishing this differ. Leader-types benefit from gaining confidence through opportunities that allow them to test drive their leadership by overseeing projects and experimenting with new ideas.

One thing we learned from effective leader-parents we interviewed for this book is that they try to have consistent, one-on-one time with their children. This allows the parent to tailor fit interactions based on the uniqueness of each child.

> **KidLead Idea:** *Sit through a classroom session with your child's teachers, or observe the way your child's coach runs the team. The goal is to assess the environment and styles of those with whom you entrust your child's development. Your child trusts you when you delegate supervision. Good teachers/coaches are not threatened by being observed. Ultimately, it's your responsibility, so assert yourself to at least watch how other adults oversee your child's development, handle discipline, and respond to the young leaders in the group. As a courtesy to the teacher and principal, set up an appointment to do this and explain that your reason is simply to observe, not that you perceive any problems or have heard any complaints.*

3. Intimidating with threats and verbal warnings. ("I'm the boss around here.")

If you've ever walked down the aisle at Wal-Mart or your local grocery store, you've probably heard a parent aggressively scolding a child who is misbehaving. You'll hear threats of punishment and irate responses from a parent who feels out of control. If you've ever seen the television show *Super Nanny,* you've seen examples of parents' lives being managed by budding leaders running amuck.

We've all been there as parents, hanging on to the end of our rope after a long day at work or herding kids. But when this parenting style becomes your default mode, chances are, you're diminishing the leadership abilities of your children. This is most common among two types of parents: parents who are not leaders themselves but have leader-type kids, and parents who are leaders but who lack sufficient emotional intelligence to handle an immature leader trying to stretch his or her wings. The result is butting heads. The parents feel overwhelmed. In order to diminish the young leader's power, they try to intimidate with verbal or physical force. The goal is tension reduction.

Helping young leaders gain confidence and self-discipline is a difficult process. It requires very intentional concentration on saying and doing the right things at strategic times called teachable moments. These are situations of failure, conflict, and discipline, where you are able to attach consequences to actions and attitudes. Don't rush the process if possible. Push "pause" and discuss the various parts or perceptions leading up to the situation. When you play the "parent card" in order to gain control and get your way, it usually means you've lost the battle. This is a last resort strategy. When this becomes your standard mode of parenting, your child has lost the opportunity to develop his or her leadership potential while living in your home. Leaders, more than others, want to feel respected for what they bring to the table and acknowledged for their ideas. They need a safe place to express their gifts of influence, where they can grow in confidence and fail with dignity.

4. Punishing vs. disciplining a creative and strong-willed child.

While all dads are men, not all men are dads. The same logic goes for leaders. While most leaders possess strong wills, not all strong-willed kids are leaders. Therefore, handling a strong-willed leader may appear to be simply a parenting issue, but it is more than that. In the beginning of this chapter, we told the story of a middle-aged man who grew up with a dominant father whose overbearing parenting style stunted the young leader's development. While this leader was at home, he was very quiet and passive, but outside of the home, he was outgoing, clownish, and a student leader at school. Punishment discourages a child from expressing his or her basic personality. Discipline hones it so that it is appropriate. Punishment strives to extinguish a behavior with pain, physical or emotional. But for the most part, punishment is fear-oriented and temporary, primarily effective only when the threat of pain is present.

When you intimidate with verbal threats or punish kids exhibiting outgoing creativity, you damage their leadership development. When this happens with kids under age fourteen, you'll usually find a child who becomes passive at home, wearing an emotional mask to survive around a parent. When this happens with youth over fourteen, you'll usually have parent-child contention and ultimately rebellion in the home. The young leader can't wait to exit the house and often does so as soon as possible with minimal looking back.

Discipline, as opposed to punishment, has to do with self-awareness, self-control, and learning the reality of consequences. A primary reason why pastors have affairs, politicians take bribes, and business leaders cut illegal deals is because these leaders failed to learn self-discipline. These individuals failed to develop self-discipline early on in life, before their characters solidified. That is why it is so important to teach kids ethical behavior. After our moral compass is set, we're far less apt to adopt values and principles that differ from those we learned in childhood or as preteens. Delay of gratification is important for everyone, but it's crucial for leaders, whose decisions impact many other people and the organizations they serve.

5. Lack of intentional mentoring and training.

When a photographer sees a pastoral setting at sunset, she wants to capture it with her camera. When a coach sees an athlete with natural gifting, he wants him on the team so he can tap the talent. When a teacher finds a student with incredible promise, she creates opportunities to challenge the pupil. People look for opportunities like these all the time. But what do we do when we see a young child with natural leadership gifts? Most of the time, we do nothing. At best, we say, "Someday, you're going to be a leader." Ignoring a child's unique gift of influence can retard his or her progress if we miss key developmental periods. That is why we've invested so much time and energy into *Lead*Now, a program that we've designed for ten- to thirteen-year-olds.

> ***KidLead Idea:*** *If you dare, rate yourself on these five behaviors. How do you measure up on a 1-4 scale (1-I realize I've been doing this quite a bit, 2-I see that I resort to some of these behaviors from time to time, 3-I could improve but I'm doing pretty well, 4-I think I'm doing a good job avoiding these items)? Better yet, why not let your 8- to 18-year-old read this chapter and then give you some feedback?*

Why Adults Fail to Develop Young Leaders

Parents and adults overlook intentional mentoring and training due to a few common reasons. One is that they don't recognize leadership indicators. As we've mentioned, parents confuse leadership aptitude with being rebellious, strong-willed, bossy, opinionated, overly confident, or outgoing. Some misperceive academic excellence with leading. Misdiagnosis is dangerous in medicine as well as child development. While we have programs such as youth athletics, arts, and academics that reveal aptitude in these areas, we rarely find venues for assessing leadership aptitude. Leaders, therefore, don't see these abilities in themselves as students until they look back as adults.

Another is that they assume leadership development will emerge later on its own. Because our culture believes that leading is an adult activity, we perceive it is not our responsibility to develop latent talent. Instead, we assume that we've done our work by merely raising our kids responsibly and getting them to college or their first job. Then it's life or Corporate America that will train them how to lead. Thus, we procrastinate leadership development among children and youth.

Yet another reason is that they don't have the skills needed to differentiate leader development from normal parenting and teaching. That is the reason for this book. We want to help parents, teachers, and coaches develop their abilities in detecting, developing, and deploying young leaders. Most of us have never seen leadership development skills modeled when we were young, let alone received any formal training regarding youth leadership development.

One more reason adults overlook developing budding leaders is that they lack adequate tools, programs, and resources designed to hone both character and competencies. Most programs calling themselves leadership are really more about parenting, community service, self-esteem, and character. Up to now, nearly all serious leadership programs and resources have focused on adults. Those with a youth emphasis tend to be generic programs that fail to distinguish those children with natural aptitude.

When a parent sees that his child has exceptional soccer ability, he will try to find a club or competitive team where the level of play and coaching will likely develop the child's potential. Chances are it will cost more time and money, but recreational soccer leagues will not help the child improve significantly. The same is true whether it is sports, arts, science, or any number of other unique gifts and abilities. This is the reason for AP classes and Gifted and Talented programs in schools, to provide special development opportunities for academic success. Leadership should be no different.

Good News

History is full of stories of young leaders who were overlooked, misunderstood, and had any inclination of leadership beaten out of them, sometimes literally. Many children gifted as leaders are wrongly diagnosed and defeated by well-intentioned adults who either do not understand their unique wiring or fail to know what to do with it when it is exhibited.

Far too many resources flow toward fixing social problems. They are reactionary in nature, consuming billions of dollars and hundreds of thousands of hours. Leadership development, especially among young leaders, is primarily preventative. If we identified and proactively trained young leaders, we'd reduce the number of gang leaders, curtail future CEO scandals, and decrease organizational floundering that results when leaders go bad. Besides that, more and better leaders would address the remaining problems with greater confidence and diligence. We invest far too much effort on squeaky wheels in society, wondering why we seem to make little headway over the long haul.

The good news is that the more we become aware of leadership aptitude in children, avoid behaviors that limit them, and pursue methods to develop them positively, the more we'll raise the quality and quantity of leaders. We'll reduce the amount of tension that influencers cause when they lack character and competencies. We'll have more effective and ethical leaders for our corporations, communities, and civic organizations. We believe history has yet to see some of the finest examples of leadership, as we begin to seriously develop those gifted in leading, early in life, while they're impressionable.

Truett Cathy, founder of Chick-fil-A, tells KidLead
about his views on leading early.

If you want to raise a leader, you need to set an example first. Federal law doesn't permit a kid to work until he's sixteen, but I started when I was eight. Teaching kids how to work is very important. Keep them busy. When I look over a résumé of a thirty-five-year-old, I look for leadership ability early and see if they're a high achiever.

When I was young, someone gave me a book by Napoleon Hill called Think and Grow Rich. It taught me that anything you can conceive and believe, you can achieve. I had a low image of myself because I wasn't an outstanding student. We need to start early. You can't wait until they're teenagers. Give them responsibility. I didn't let my children have a car until they were eighteen. I started telling them that when they were ten and eleven, so they didn't get to thirteen thinking I'd give them a car by sixteen. I let my kids drive our cars, but they were responsible for buying their own after they turned eighteen.

And don't forget to give your kids quality time. Take each child on a date or out to eat, one- on-one, at least once a month. Let them know you care. It is also important who they associate with and that you help them grow spiritually. I've taught a thirteen-year-old boys' Sunday school class for over fifty years.

Discussion Activators

1. By becoming aware of our past, we can improve the way we come across to our children. Share a time in your childhood when an adult in your past broke your spirit by something s/he said or did.

2. Did any of these five behaviors surprise you? If so, which one(s)?

3. If you were to add another item to this list of five, what would it be?

4. Share a time or way that you may have thwarted your young leader by doing one of these five things. How do you want to improve?

If you want to train leaders you have to start early, but it isn't easily done. We have to conduct research, educate a wider public, and mobilize citizen allies. We have to persuade diverse groups to work together—schools, social agencies, the faith community, law enforcement, all levels of government and so on.

- John W. Gardner

Chapter 4
The 10/13 Window

A Time to Plant

Planting crops in the Midwest where I grew up can be precarious. If you begin too early, chances are, a freeze will kill the fragile sprouts. If you begin too late, the crop won't mature sufficiently for harvest; the first freeze will abruptly end its development. There is a window when farmers must get the seed in the ground if they want to reap a good crop in autumn. The same is true of leadership. This window for leaders to learn ethical leadership is precariously positioned in four critical years, from ages ten to thirteen.

Strong, virtuous character is vital for effective, ethical leadership. History primarily consists of good leaders staying good, good leaders going bad, and evil leaders behaving badly. Outside of significant inventions (e.g., Guttenberg press, penicillin, airplane, computer) and disease/disasters (e.g., bubonic plague, Mount Vesuvius, malaria, influenza), a majority of history centers on the rise and fall of civilizations at the hands of adventurers and political and military leaders.

Even today, we are besieged with news events regarding leaders gone wild, who cook the books, shaft investors, and let their egos get in the way of good judgment. The majority suffers from the decisions of a few. That is the downside of leadership. Most of us have worked for an unethical leader who tiptoed through mine fields, eventually creating a debris field of hurting people and organizational chaos. Perhaps as a leader you've done some things in the past that you'd like to undo. You know the challenge of effective, ethical leading firsthand. These failures usually find their roots in inadequate preparation during key times as children, when our character is molded.

Effective Leading Is Ethical Leading

Hybrid vehicles combine the technology of two energy sources, typically an internal combustion engine and an electric motor. When you're driving, you often cannot detect whether you're using gas or electricity as the vehicle switches back and forth between the two. This serves as a metaphor for ethical leadership. The goal is to develop leaders who are so grounded in good character that they don't hesitate when making ethical choices while leading. Their inner compass directs them toward true north, so they consistently make decisions that bring value to others and benefit society as a whole.

Even ethical leaders have to wrestle over decisions that create loss, regardless of the choice made. Do we lay off employees or reduce stockholders' profits? Do we cut a deal that is legal but goes against some of our organizational values, even though it would be profitable? Issues like these litter the daily schedules and sometimes the nighttime sleep of leaders around the world.

But far too much wrestling takes place over issues that should be simple because the ethical components essential to good leading dictate it. High standards make leading easier in that we are less distracted by issues that should be clean cut, allowing us to tend to other important matters. Figuring out how to connive, cheat, deceive, and cover up are ultimately taxing.

Leaders make decisions in part based on who they are as people and also how they think in terms of values and standards. This is referred to as character. Therefore, we should all be concerned about the character of a leader and his or her internal compass.

Some like to think *who* a leader is as a person has little to do with *how* s/he functions. Unfortunately, this is not the case over the long haul. Rarely will a leader take personal commitments lightly while taking corporate commitments seriously. If you go back on your word with your family, you're apt to do it with colleagues. If you cheat on the golf course, you're likely to cut corners in the boardroom. Ultimately, you cannot separate who you are as a person from how you operate as a leader. A leader's character unconsciously impacts his or her decision making.

Compartmentalizing is the process whereby we separate our lives into a variety of non-overlapping areas. People separate their personal lives from their public lives when they use different standards on the job than they use at home. Compartmentalizing seems to work for some, but it rarely works for leaders. While we can point to examples of leaders who seemed to cheat their way to the top or maintained a dark side with few consequences, these are extreme exceptions.

What we crave are leaders who naturally make ethical decisions. Getting this kind of leadership requires that we start early.

> ***KidLead Idea:*** *Invite your child to do mini-reports on 4 leaders, such as Mahatma Gandhi, Abraham Lincoln, Adolf Hitler, Joseph Stalin, or some other combination you prefer. Select two known to be ethical and two known to be unethical. Offer to pay them to write a 1-page overview of each person's life and have them answer the question: Was this leader a good leader or a bad leader? If your child is too young, then look up the bios yourself on www.Wikipedia.org. (Remember, "pay" doesn't necessarily mean money. Reward desired behavior.)*

Return on Investment of the 10/13 Window

When you plot cognitive development with moral development, there's a strategic overlap that is easier to understand when presented visually as in the following graph.

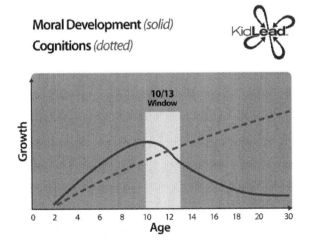

Moral Development *(solid)*
Cognitions *(dotted)*

KidLead

The solid line in the graph represents moral development, such as character, values, and the way we determine right from wrong. This begins around the age of two and crescendos between nine and thirteen years of age. By fourteen, our moral fabric is pretty much established. Even though we learn to articulate our standards and philosophy better throughout teen years and early adulthood, we are not likely to change significantly, outside of traumatic experiences that mark us. These include painful consequences of failure, confronting life and death, counseling, or a spiritual epiphany of sorts. Therefore, a typical leader's character is pretty much determined before s/he has any formal training or experience at leading.

Moral psychologists such as Kohlberg agree that much of our moral fiber has been established before high school. When you look at history and civilizations around the world, you'll notice that the rites of passage to adulthood usually take place between the ages of twelve and fourteen. Whether it's Confirmation, Bar Mitzvah or Bat Mitzvah, a *walkabout* for an Australian Aborigine, or other formal or informal ceremonies, most societies acknowledge what modern psychologists have recently discovered, that adult character is pretty much established by fourteen years of age.

Following numerous corporate debacles in the 1970s, graduate business schools began adding ethics courses to their programs. While such training looks great, for the most part it's window dressing. The reason is that by graduate school, our character is pretty much established. By college and high school, our moral fiber has gelled, even though our ability to articulate it verbally increases.

The dotted line in the graphic represents our cognitive development. This also emerges around age two, but it crescendos around thirty-five. Piaget and others who've studied cognitive development acknowledge a distinct change around age ten. Even though children are still very concrete in their thinking at this milestone, they can begin to understand concepts when they are put in the context of an actual experience. During our prototyping of KidLead training, we found this to be true as well.

Before age ten, it is difficult to teach leadership because it is both a concept as well as a somewhat complicated social behavior. But from ten and up, you can teach leadership, especially to those with an aptitude to learn leading. As we noted, most leadership training does not take place until the ages of twenty-five to thirty-five, when adults are employed by corporations that need better leaders and can pay for formal coaching as well as on-the-job mentoring. Some leadership training and opportunities exist for college students and a handful for high schoolers. The problem is that by this time, moral development is pretty much over.

Some may ask, "Can kids at this age really learn how to lead?" I was skeptical myself. As we developed the original concept of *Lead*Now training for ten- to thirteen-year-olds, I was hesitant because I thought it might be just another youth activity, similar to any number of after school or extracurricular programs that parents might use to keep their kids busy. After all, I was an adult who was serious about leadership development. Why should I be interested in kids? But I have discovered that they can lead. In fact, in the right setting and with the right curriculum and coaching, ten- to thirteen-year-olds learn faster and more effectively than adults. They have less to unlearn and fewer distractions that preoccupy teens and adults.

Steve Grant is a Certified KidLead Trainer who provides adult leadership training for corporations around the country. He comments, "These kids learn faster than adults who are fresh out of MBA programs. They're able to articulate concepts and think original thoughts, so you know they're not just parroting what they're taught. It's exciting to see." What it comes down to is ROI, return on investment. Even though we invest billions of dollars annually in adult leadership development, we'd get better results if we invested in leaders while they were moldable.

Kate Thomesen synthesizes the neurological importance of this period.

> During early adolescence, around the ages of 11 to 12 years, the brain undergoes two processes known as "blossoming" and "pruning." Blossoming is the huge growth spurt of dendrites (nerve cell endings that receive information and transmit nerve impulses). Pruning removes dendrites that are not used (or hard-wired) into the brain. Experience causes the brain to activate neurons (nerve cells). When the neurons are activated over and over, they become hard-wired in

the brain. The hard-wiring indicates that a person has developed a skill.[1]

The potential power of providing executive-level training for budding leaders while they're in their preteen years is significant. Imagine what it would be like if twenty-five- to thirty-five-year- olds came to their leader roles in organizations with fifteen to twenty-five years of experience in leading. That's a big head start. **The 10/13 Window is critical because it represents the four years when cognitions are sufficiently developed to comprehend leadership concepts, and character is still pliable.**

> **KidLead Idea:** *A quick way to communicate this concept is to ask adults to hold a small ball of modeling clay or Play-Doh in one hand and a similar sized rock or dried piece of clay in the other. Then squeeze. The soft substance represents a young character that is still pliable, moldable, and the hard substance illustrates when our character is set.*

Combining Character with Competencies

Honesty, honor, integrity, servanthood, commitment, and responsibility are vital qualities in leading. History is full of examples of influential leaders who lacked these core qualities. The results were war, torture, thievery, bribery, and every heinous crime imaginable. Because character is so important for effective leading, learning leadership in the context of ethics is essential. When we interweave character issues with skills, we increase the likelihood these won't be separated during leading. We should not assume leaders possess these qualities or understand how they apply to real-world situations.

Look at it this way. I have a set of tools that allow me to work on my car, but just because I know my tools doesn't mean I know how to fix my vehicle. If someone shows me how to use my tools on my car, I'm more likely to succeed. When family members, coaches, and educators

1   Thomesen, Kate. *Parenting Preteens with a Purpose*. Minneapolis: Search Institute Press, 2008 (34-35).

model and teach character issues, they are giving children a valuable set of tools they can use throughout life. But understanding how these tools work in the setting of leading others is also important. We should not assume the knowledge of tools automatically translates into all settings. Leadership trainers should not presume that these tools needed to lead are present.

This is where skills and ethics intersect. Good leadership development focuses on this intersection because when it fails to do this, collisions will occur. When you entrust people who lack character with power, you will have problems. As the saying goes, "Power corrupts and absolute power corrupts absolutely." When we teach skills that heighten the ability to influence but ignore character issues or fail to teach them when leaders are moldable, we will be disappointed by the results. No wonder smart, savvy, charismatic, and intelligent people still implode by making stupid mistakes that are character-oriented. Leadership, more than any role in society, exposes and challenges character weaknesses. Were it a private experience, it would matter little. But when leaders fail, the ripple effect impacts many.

Action Plan

The primary reason we lack effective, ethical leaders is not because of inadequate adult leadership training. Organizations, books, courses, and trainers abound for them. We will continue to lack sufficient leaders for the future until we intentionally focus on training leaders while they are pliable as preteens. I believe that training preteens as leaders is the most overlooked natural resource in the world. That is why we've focused on leadership development resources for ten- to thirteen-year-olds, and this is why we encourage you to do the same.

If you are a parent of a child younger than fourteen, you still have time to focus on character and moral development. The more you can do this in the context of leading, the better your young leader will be at combining the two as s/he gets older. If you missed the window to teach both character and leadership at the same time, then focus on teaching skills that have a character component to them and intentionally talk about them in hopes of raising awareness. You are not likely to significantly change what you've already planted. Life and its consequences will be your child's primary character instructor from this point. **Lead**Well is the program we use for fourteen- to eighteen-year-olds. It is very similar to **Lead**Now, for ten- to thirteen-year-olds, but we realize that teens will develop leadership skills more than character, since moral training is significantly less productive after thirteen.

If we focus on leadership development during the 10/13 Window, we'll see scores of more effective and ethical leaders than in the past.

> Les Parrott III, PhD, psychologist, bestselling author of *3 Seconds*, and founder of RealRelationships.com, tells KidLead about his dad's influence on him.
>
> When I was in the eighth grade, my dad offered me five dollars to read a book called *Total Commitment*. As a youngster, that money got my attention, and I started reading the book that very day. Truth be told, it could have been an offer to read the phonebook as far as I was concerned. But what started as a monetary motivation soon turned into a genuine interest in the subject. The book contained the stories of twenty leaders who attributed much of their success to what Benjamin Disraeli called "constancy of purpose." Each of these stories—whether it was Alonzo Decker of the Black & Decker Manufacturing Company or the great track athlete Jesse Owens—demonstrated to me, as a young kid, that to enjoy longstanding achievement I would need to cultivate the kind of commitment each of them had found. Dad and I talked throughout my school days—even into college—about the stories in this book that he and I had read some thirty years ago. We had another animated conversation on the subject this very year, when he and mom gave me a long-lost copy of this book that had inspired me as a kid to be a leader. What a gift! It's one of the most tangible things my parents did to develop my leadership potential.

Discussion Activators

1. Discuss situations where timing is important, whether it's planting a garden, making a sale, or some other situation where outcomes are directly related to taking action during temporary conditions. Relate this to the 10/13 window.

2. If you were a lawyer or debater presenting the importance of character training as a part of leadership training, what would you say?

3. Why do you think our culture has all but overlooked serious leadership training for ten- to thirteen-year-olds?

4. What was one thing that provoked your thinking in this chapter?

Section II.

⌘ ⌘ ⌘

Developing Young Leaders: Skills

To not reach our goals is not a sin; to not dream is. When it comes to preteens, let us not be guilty of low aim.

-David Satcher, M.D., Ph.D. (16th U.S. Surgeon General)

Chapter 5

Eight Ways to Grow Leaders

There are three common situations where young leaders fail to be developed. One is where a non-leader-parent, -teacher, or -coach fails to recognize leadership aptitude in a child or misdiagnoses it as a rebellious attitude. A second is where a leader-parent, -teacher, or -coach overwhelms the young leader, is unwilling to share power, and intimidates the budding leader into compliance. The third scenario is where both non-leader and leader recognize leadership ability in a child but don't know how to develop it. They hope that someone, someday, somehow will recognize and unleash the latent potential in the young influencer.

The good news is that whether you're a leader or not, you can grow the young leaders around you. That is the big idea of this book. In this chapter, you'll discover eight practical ways to begin doing this. While these are best suited for parents or guardians, others who work with young leaders can adapt them. We'll give educators specific ideas for creating leader-friendly classrooms in Chapter 8.

Influencer Grooming

1. Look at your child as a young leader.

See his or her potential. Leadership development of your child begins between your ears, how you think about him or her. As a parent, you will be the most influential person in the life of your child, at least until college and often beyond. Therefore, while you want to enjoy your children at every stage of their development, imagine them grown up. See your child as a person who someone will someday hire, marry, and who will influence others. All too often, we love our children but limit them by the way we see them. We continue to picture them as the helpless babes they were when we first met them, thus overlooking their unique strengths and aptitudes.

One of the benefits we've seen in **Lead***Now* training modules is that the Certified Trainers and *Koaches* (our term for adult team coaches) often do not know the *Leaders* (our term for ten- to thirteen-year-old participants) very well. That means we don't see them as kids. We visualize them as future CEOs, presidents, community activists, and entrepreneurs. Because our culture considers leading primarily as an adult activity, most parents rarely see the ability of their children to lead as young people. As we stated earlier in the book, parents want to look at your child's abilities and aptitudes. If one of them seems to be leading, then the next step is not about them, it's about how YOU think about them.

2. Treat your child as a young leader.

The reason why we need to begin seeing our children as leaders is because this will directly affect how we treat them. How we treat them influences how they see themselves and, as a result, how they react. This is known as the Pygmalion effect, which says that people become as they are treated. The term refers to a story from Greek mythology, based on the name of a sculptor who crafted an ivory statue of a beautiful woman. He treated the sculpture as if it were alive, giving it gifts, dressing it with a necklace, and caressing it. After saying a prayer to the goddess Aphrodite, she turned the sculpture into a live woman, whom Pygmalion then married.

When we begin treating our children as leaders, we'll see them respond as leaders, especially when they exhibit leadership aptitude. "Alexa, you're a leader. How would a good leader respond in this situation?" "Jason, I want you to be a leader when your friends come over, so what can you do to organize some activities?" Obviously, merely calling your child a leader is insufficient, but as you begin providing opportunities that support your words, you will see behavior change. This is one of the most amazing transformations we see after just a few training sessions in **Lead***Now*, where the preteen Leaders are expected to lead their peers in activities that begin to change their self-images and thus their speech and behavior.

KidLead Idea: Rent the movie, <u>My Fair Lady</u>, which is a film depiction of <u>Pygmalion</u> by George Bernard Shaw. Note how Professor Higgins watches the street urchin Eliza Doolittle transform into a lady because he treats her as one. Then plan how you can change the way you respond to your child as a leader.

3. Develop at-home opportunities to lead.

You can, with a little tweaking, transform everyday activities into leadership training opportunities. We'll provide an entire chapter on this later (Chapter 7). The main point is that you can give your child a big head start in leadership by transitioning from parent to leadership coach in any number of ongoing chores and events.

4. Discuss leadership situations as they arise from school, news, movies, and work.

Nearly everyday, you'll have life events, stories, and media that provide opportunities to talk about leadership, whether in brief sound bytes or more prolonged discussions. The goal is to make your child aware of situations where leaders influence others—for good and for bad—in order to create an unconscious orientation so that they can "read" leadership situations. For example, let's say that your child comes home from school and tells you about a food fight that broke out in the cafeteria.

"It was amazing," Cyndi says. "Bobby Nanson and Jonny Carol started throwing french fries at each other. Then a whole bunch of people started tossing things from their lunches. Then the principal walked in and got really mad. He made a lot of people stay after school and clean up the lunch room."

As a parent, you could say something such as, "My goodness. You didn't throw any food, did you?" Or you might react, "That's terrible. It's a good thing they got in trouble."

But if you changed hats from parent to leadership coach, you might respond, "So why do you think the other kids started throwing food? Do you think they did it just because Bobby and Jonny did? Do kids follow Bobby and Jonny in other situations, like in class or the playground?" If the answer is "yes," then ask, "Why do you think they follow them?" "Do you think their decision to start throwing food was a good one or not?" "Why do you think that?"

The goal is neutral, matter-of-fact conversation, helping your child begin thinking about social influencers and raising his or her awareness of leadership situations.

In another scenario, you're driving home from the movie *Shrek 2* with your child and a few friends. You might ask, "What do you think about the scene when the King met Shrek? How did the King treat Shrek? How do you think the King's response made Shrek feel? Why is a leader's response to people so important?"

Notice that you're not lecturing, condemning, criticizing, or giving answers. You're asking strategic questions. In our KidLead Trainer Certification, we teach trainers not to talk more than 25 percent of the time during Team Time discussions. This is the period after an activity when the team debriefs to discuss the concept being learned as well as how the team functioned. One thing we've discovered, especially among ten- and eleven-year-olds, is that they expect the adult to have the answer and do most of the talking. But after a few club meetings, when the preteens are asked questions and given unrushed time to talk, they gain confidence and begin sharing their ideas.

Here's one more scenario. You're with your daughter but talking on your phone with a colleague about a situation at work that your boss seems to be handling poorly. You don't like it that a few individuals seem to be getting away with working less, requiring you and your partners to cover their responsibilities, while your supervisor turns his head. After you hang up from the call, you say nothing or you mutter with disgust, "That's so unfair. Our boss isn't doing his job."

You could also turn to your daughter, briefly explain the situation, and then ask questions, such as: "What do you think about that?" "What do you think we should do?" "Have you ever had a teacher or coach who didn't seem to be treating everyone the same?" "Why do you think leaders do that?" And if you're really confident, you can ask, "Can you think of a time when I treated you that way or gave preferred treatment to your brother or sister? If so, when was it and how could I improve?"

What you're doing is communicating the idea that leaders aren't perfect but can learn. Leaders must become aware of others' feelings and treat people on their teams fairly, or at least explain why someone may or may not be carrying as much of the workload. You are also teaching your child, whether you realize it or not, how to *lead up*, influencing those with greater authority and power. If you act like a victim, then you're training your child to be a complainer. If you are taking a proactive, assertive approach to addressing the situation, you're showing her how she can influence positively even if she's not the boss.

Everyday, situations arise in your family members' lives and in the media that create teachable moments when you can initiate mini-discussions about leaders and how people influence each other. You may not always get a lot of response from your children, but don't underestimate the benefit of them thinking about what you say and learning how to analyze a leadership situation.

> **KidLead Idea:** *While this concept is still fresh, brainstorm a recent movie, TV show, work or family event you recently experienced from which you could unpack a leadership issue with your child. Keep it simple, but get started by writing it down now.*

Steve Grant, leadership consultant and KidLead Certified Trainer

It took many years for me to realize that when my daughters ask a question, they don't necessarily want my answer. If I did answer their question, they'd respond, "You never listen," or "You just don't understand me." So I stopped answering and started asking questions. It went something like this: "Dad, which dress do you like best?" I would then respond, "How do you feel about each one?" She would then give me several reasons for liking or not liking the dress. I listened intently to what she said and then just summarized her thoughts. "It sounds like you think it might be too formal and it's a more casual dance. Plus the color just isn't right for you, so perhaps you should wear the other dress that you feel more comfortable in and is a better color for you." My daughter would smile and say, "Thanks, Daddy. I knew you would know what to wear." Leaders help others discover solutions, but they don't always give them the answer. Leaders value the thoughts and opinions of others.

5. Find opportunities for leading in the community.

Creating leadership projects in the home can naturally evolve into similar situations in the community. This is where a budding leader can gain significant confidence. As you begin getting into the neighborhood and organizations with which you're familiar, you also help other adults grasp the idea that child and youth leaders can make a significant difference on their own.

Begin with organizations where you and/or your child have familiarity. This might be a church or synagogue, school, ball team, or immediate neighborhood. Talk with the adult in charge (pastor, rabbi, priest, principal, coach, or city official) and ask about needs or small projects that could use a hand. Most nonprofits have a variety of small tasks that get overlooked at any given time. Your question may catch the people in charge off guard, so you may need to brainstorm ideas with them or perhaps ask them to think about it. Obviously, you need to keep in mind the age of the child, the difficulty of the project, and what it might take to accomplish the tasks. You'll want to begin small as your young leader gains confidence.

The key, as in all leadership projects, is that you have a clear objective, that there are multiple people involved, and that you truly let your child lead, as opposed to telling him or her what to do and then merely calling the task leadership.

In **Lead***Now*, preteens have led others in collecting school supplies for needy kids, raising money for a child advocacy home, organizing recycling drives in schools, and convincing a principal to change school policy due to a bully causing havoc on the playground. We have more ideas on projects like these at the KidLead website (www.kidlead. com). Unless you have someone from the organization supervising the project, you may need to be available to serve as a coach, who may or may not choose to be on the team. You'll be tempted to take over at times and tell the leaders what to do, but try to avoid this unless a decision relates to safety issues. We'll talk more about coaching skills in the next chapter.

A growing number of schools require community service from their students. This is a wonderful trend that helps young people experience giving back, without pay, to those in need. The big difference between most community service opportunities and leadership training is that the former are done as individuals or followers. But when a young leader organizes and supervises peers and even adults, they learn about leading.

Again, make sure that you provide feedback times at the end when youth can think about what went well, what didn't go well, and what they might improve next time. Articulating what did and didn't go well, how people worked together, and other aspects of the project takes learning to a much higher level.

> **KidLead Idea:** *While this concept is still fresh, brainstorm a project that you could initiate with an organization, or write the name of someone you can talk to who might have ideas of small projects that a team led by your child could accomplish.*

6. Introduce your child to other leaders.

Leaders recognize other leaders. A child with leadership aptitude will have a certain amount of natural affinity with other leaders regardless of their age. When you are meeting someone who is a leader in his or her organization or field, go out of your way to have your child meet this person. While many parents still exhibit the "children should be seen, not heard" attitude, at least when it comes to meeting people of power and organizational importance, this anxiety is based more on their own insecurity. I've found that most leaders do well meeting children, especially kids with leadership aptitude, because adult leaders see it in them as well. Adult leaders feel honored, and the really good ones focus on the child, looking her eye to eye and shaking her hand. You know when you've met a good leader when s/he gets down to your child's eye level and begins conversing with the young leader, ignoring you for the moment.

In one situation reported in the Bible, Jesus scolded his handlers for keeping the children away from him. He said, "Hey, let the kids come to me. I want to meet them. You can learn a lot from them." When our oldest son, Jeff, was a junior in college, he was thinking about becoming a psychologist. At the time, I was interviewing a bestselling author who was a psychologist, for a magazine I worked for as executive editor. I called Jeff and said, "I'm meeting with Dr. Cloud. Would like you to drop by for five minutes and meet him?"

I purchased one of Dr. Cloud's books and introduced him to Jeff. He autographed the book for Jeff, and I took their picture as they talked briefly. The whole episode took less than five minutes, but it was a way of esteeming Jeff as well as introducing him to a leader in his field of interest. We've done this dozens of times over the years as opportunities have arisen. While it often requires pre-thinking and a little extra organization, the results are worth it.

Obviously, you need to be sensitive to both your child and the leader you want him to meet. It may be appropriate to ask the leader's permission or say, "I'd love to have my son meet you briefly, if that's okay." Again, this type of invitation is seen more as an honor than a burden for most leaders. Savvy leaders are good at the politics of relationships; they understand that family ties and friendships are important parts of getting things done, and they know the importance of conveying that they are approachable, friendly, and humble. Good leaders accomplish this with authenticity.

> **KidLead Idea:** *Think of a leader you know at your work to whom you can introduce your child. Consider taking your child to work for a day, so s/he can see what you do and meet your colleagues and/or boss. KidLead Trainer, Steve Grant, provides another work variation. "For years we've been doing an annual 'bring your child to work' program. But instead of merely boring the kids with watching us work, we do a leadership activity. We divide the kids into teams, and the company gives each team $200, along with a list of approved charities. Each team has to decide what charity will receive its money. This teaches negotiation skills."*

7. Help your child find a mentor.

All of us as parents are limited in what we can provide for our children when it comes to modeling and communicating experiences. The statement is well-worn but true: "It takes a village to raise a child." One thing parents can do to nurture their young leaders is help them find mentors who lead in different organizations and with varying styles. We'll discuss mentoring in more depth in Chapter 9.

8. Seek formal and informal leadership training.

When we detect musical talent, we get our child music lessons. When we discern academic ability, we move them toward AP classes and Gifted and Talented programs. When we observe athletic ability, we hire coaching from a pro and seek competitive-level teams. The challenge most parents face when they see leadership aptitude in their child is finding any semblance of concentrated leadership training. Very little exists that teaches leader character and skills. We've found a few at the high school and college level but little to nothing specifically designed for the 10/13 Window, which is why we created **Lead***Now*.

Analyzing a Program Deemed to be "Leadership"

If you do not have a **Lead***Now* or **Lead***Well* program in your area, here are five questions when analyzing a program deemed to be leadership, since merely calling something leadership does not make it such.

1. What's the curriculum?

Is there anything that is written or prepared that you can review? If it is informal, are the teachers just winging it? The more intentional the training is, with content and guidelines for the trainers, the more likely it will be thought through and effective. If there is a curriculum or printed agenda, review a sample. Does it seem to be group- or team-oriented? Is it a series of classroom lectures, or are there hands-on training activities, where the students participate directly? Sitting in a study or listening to leaders give speeches is not nearly as effective as when young leaders do tasks.

2. Who designed it?

Is it a homegrown mish-mash of ideas and lessons patched together by someone who is inundated with other responsibilities, or was it designed by people who are not only leaders themselves but also have expertise in the field? What are the qualifications of the source? What are the goals of the program? Do they measure effectiveness or just assume the program accomplishes the goals?

3. Does it focus on leadership specifically?

Leadership is a very popular term. People know that if they use the word in a program or course description, it's apt to get attention. When we hear about a youth leadership program, we try to analyze its content. We've reviewed dozens. What we've found is that most "leadership" programs are about individual character development and/or service. While these are good, they are not leadership in terms of organizing people to work toward common goals. Being a confident, serving individual is one thing. Leading others is quite a different process.

4. How are participants selected?

Again, this goes back to how you define leadership and whether or not you believe everyone can become a leader as you define it. Regardless, everyone does not have the same aptitude for leading people. Is the program based on academic success, commitment, whoever wants to pay the participant fee, or more refined screening processes? When you get young leaders with higher levels of aptitude together, you'll see different results than a "ya'll come" program. That is why academic institutions such as Harvard, Stanford, Yale, and MIT maintain high reputations in their fields.

5. Who is running the program?

How are these people selected? What is their level of experience and training in terms of leading and working with preteens or teens? Is this person a leader in the community or corporate realm, or do they simply like working with young people?

We applaud everyone attempting to develop young leaders in their homes and in their communities, but as a parent, you'll want to be knowledgeable about the quality of the program, just as you care about the school your child attends or the food s/he eats.

There are numerous ways you can assist the children in your life to develop their leadership potential. We'll give you many more, but the big idea is that it will take a little re-orientation for you as a parent, teacher, or coach if you want to germinate the seed of influence in young leaders.

> George Foreman, former Heavyweight Boxing Champion, entrepreneur, and father to ten children, tells KidLead one way he helps nurture leadership.
>
> I'll ask one child, who may be the least expecting it, to lead us in a family activity. For example, we may be at the dinner table and I'll say, "Hey, you want to ask God to bless our food for us, please?" I always put them in positions where they are leaders as soon as I can communicate with them. The next thing you know, they say, "Dad is waiting for me to lead him." They see me trying to give them my position.
>
> A lot of times you see them thinking, "I can't do it." Then I get much lower than they are so they try to help me. They begin thinking, "I'm going to help Dad." Years ago, I heard Sammy Davis Jr. say, "You've got to make them love you." If you make your kids love you, they'll do anything for you. The next thing you know, they're trying to assist me, and they feel pitiful for me. They feel like they're better at what they're doing than what I'm doing. This gives them confidence they'll need to be leaders.

Discussion Activators

1. What was a helpful idea you got from this chapter?

2. If you responded to one or more of the last three KidLead Ideas in this chapter, what ideas did you brainstorm?

3. Brainstorm as a group:

   a. A news, work or family event that you can use to talk about leadership with your child

   b. A community project your child could work on with a team or a key contact

   c. A local leader you know to whom you could introduce your child

4. What questions are percolating in your mind at this point in the book?

People make history and not the other way around. In periods where there are no leaders, society stands still. Progress occurs when courageous, skillful leaders seize the opportunity to change things for the better.

-Harry S. Truman

Chapter 6

How to Coach Future Influencers

Perhaps the biggest mistake adults make with young leaders, after failing to recognize they can lead, is bumping against the young leader's will. That is why understanding the differences between parenting and coaching a young leader is invaluable. If you apply some basic skills and adopt the attitude of a coach, you'll save yourself a lot of headaches and frustration. If anything, consider this chapter a survival guide on handling budding leaders.

Know Yours and Your Child's Leadership Styles

You don't have to be a leadership expert to recognize that there are a variety of leadership styles. While many popular personality assessments focus on four predominant temperaments, these also emerge in terms of leading styles. They are Director, Inspirer, Strategist and Collaborator. Understanding these basic styles helps adults assess themselves as well as young leaders. There is no right or wrong style. All can be effective when used properly. These are natural tendencies and typically do not change over time although leaders can vary them temporarily, depending on the situation.

Adult leaders often mistakenly assume that their leadership style is the only correct way to lead, and they try to shape young leaders to fit that mold. All four dominant styles have unique strengths and weaknesses. When we force a style unnatural to a young leader, we make him or her susceptible to displaying the weaknesses instead of the strengths, since the strengths are more difficult to adopt.

I write and eat left-handed. Fortunately my parents did not try to switch me to the right hand, but I've heard several frustrated left-handers whose teachers or parents did. Like preferred hand use, leaders have a preferred style that feels right to them. It is wise to help a young leader develop in that style and not necessarily adopt a different preferred style of someone else. This requires learning the differences among the four leadership styles and not pushing ours onto our children. To accomplish this we need to implement emotional intelligence and coaching skills as we help a young leader with a different leading style develop his or her own. The following is a summary of four common leadership styles.

Director: This style is the stereotypical leader who emerges quickly, exuding direction and confidence.

Strengths:
•Decisive: quickly chooses a preferred course
•Visionary: imagines a preferred outcome
•Bold: willing to take risks

Weaknesses:
*Bossy: can alienate others
*Isolation: may make decisions alone
*Naïve: may overlook team input

Inspirer: This style motivates followers to feel good about participating in a cause greater than themselves.

Strengths:
•Motivational: is engaging and inspiring
•Encouraging: makes people feel good about themselves
•Positive: creates hope by seeing possibilities

Weaknesses:
*Fickle: may not follow through
*Impulsive: may not consider costs
*Talker: may seek too much attention

Strategist: This style is calculating and thoughtful, more reserved in communication but well suited for problem solving.

Strengths:
•Organized: thinks in systems
•Thorough: thinks through details
•Sensitive: alert to the feelings of others

Weaknesses:
*Negative: may be fearful of failure
*Perfectionist: can procrastinate or focus on negative
*Mired: can get stuck figuring out every detail

Collaborator: This style gets along well with people and is good at reconciliation, negotiating, and team building.

Strengths:
• Relational: likes and is liked by people
• Stable: is steady and even-keeled emotionally
• Peaceful: is good at conveying balance

Weaknesses:
*Procrastinates: can be lazy
*Reticent: can resist taking risks
*Inoffensive: may avoid confrontation

As you look at the brief lists of strengths and weaknesses, what would you say is your preferred leadership style, and what is the natural style of your young leader? You may want to ask a few people who know you well for different perspectives. How is your style the same or different from your child's, and what might be some possible differences that could either cause conflict or tempt you to try and change your child's style to be more like your own? For example, I am more of a Director but my oldest son, Jeff, is more of a Collaborator. From time to time, I've been tempted to get Jeff to be more like me, to lead as a decisive visionary. But one of Jeff's strengths is his ability to get along with a lot of people, avoid unnecessary conflict, and succeed by creating relational ties.

> **KidLead Idea:** *Write your signature with the hand you don't usually use. Then write it with your normal hand. Note the quality of your signature and how it felt with each. Use this activity to teach other adults the importance of helping their children learn how to lead in their preferred style. What style would you say your leadership leans toward, and what style seems to be your child's?*

Comparing Aptitude Strengths

In addition to identifying and contrasting leadership styles, it is also helpful for parents to estimate and contrast leadership aptitude strengths. The reason is that when there is a mismatch in terms of natural capacity between you and your child, there will naturally be tension issues unless you consciously adapt.

In the beginning of this book, we discussed leadership aptitude, a young person's natural capacity to learn how to lead. During our KidLead trainer certification, we show trainers how to estimate aptitude on a one to five scale. Applicants with a one or two value are encouraged to wait for further development, lest they not benefit sufficiently from the training. Those determined to be a three are said to be "on the bubble," meaning they may or may not be invited to participate, pending the number of Trainers and Koaches in the club and the level of other applicants' aptitudes. Those most likely to be invited into the training are fours and fives because they can make the most of the training.

While it may sound logical to suggest that those with lower numbers could benefit more, this is not the case, because capacity to learn tends to coincide with our natural strengths. Every person only has a few strengths. As we've mentioned, the responsibility of adults is to help children and youth discover and develop these individual aptitudes.

Leader strength varies among adults as well, but by adulthood, we've usually had sufficient opportunities to lead, so our capacity is better revealed. Generally, we exude a certain level of leadership.

Think of it in terms of a thermos that holds influence. Some people are smaller in the amount of their influence, others are medium, and some are able to hold a lot. On a one to five scale, one being low and five being high, what would you say is your leadership strength?

Determining the degree of your strength and the aptitude of a child is important because the difference impacts how you coach a young leader. An adult with a higher degree of leadership strength can easily intimidate a child, creating fear. The adult may discourage the young leader and make the youth feel that s/he is not good enough. Strong leaders can bowl over and push people without knowing it. Their very presence can be imposing even if they throttle back their verbal commands and directions.

Just as a parent who was an outstanding college athlete may not understand why his child isn't hitting homeruns in little league, a strong leader can have too high of expectations for a young leader and stunt his growth. If your overall leadership strength is higher, you'll need to consciously throttle back your energy so that you don't overpower the young leader.

Conversely, if you have lower leader strength than your child's capacity, the weakness will be in not challenging her sufficiently. You'll be reticent when your preteen or teen needs more push. You may not think of situations where your child can gain leading experience because you're not inclined to come up with these intuitively. You'll need to intentionally throttle up the way you coach, speak of leadership, and encourage your child to lead. When it comes to the test of wills, stand strong. Don't let your budding leader overwhelm you, lest you lose her respect. Strong leaders need pushback at times. While it feels awkward at the moment, they admire you more than if you give into them.

All our sons play or played competitive tennis. When they were starting, I coached them, and I was better than they were. But there came a point when they began beating me. While I could keep hitting with them and taking them through drills, they'd surpassed my ability to coach them sufficiently. That's when we had to take them to teaching pros and line up superior players for practice.

Unless you are a skilled leader-coach or a strong leader yourself, it will be difficult to develop a young leader whose capacity to lead is greater than your own. Your support at some point will come by getting them connected with more dynamic training, mentoring, and experiences so they can develop more fully. Your emotional support is always vital, but it's important that you estimate your own limits as well as your child's.

> **KidLead Idea:** *What would you estimate your overall leadership strength and you child's leadership aptitude to be on a 1 to 5 scale, 1 being low and 5 being high?*

The Fine Art of Disciplining a Young Leader

An important goal of developing a young leader is to help him or her become self-disciplined. This objective equips young leaders to handle power effectively. This is important for all children but vital in the life of a leader. When inner strength is missing, leaders succumb to power when sufficiently tempted. The consequences hurt them and the people they serve. Here are some ideas that are parent-oriented but pertain specifically to raising leaders.

1. Keep the rules simple.
Scores of miniscule regulations about eating, talking, cleaning, toys, television, and relationships are confusing. They can also turn kids into legalists who, when faced with situations without laws, will lack the ability to make ethical decisions. Leaders who learn rules over values are apt to finding loopholes and ways around rules that may get them and their organizations into trouble as adults. Teach values and then help them identify situations where these come into play. For example, in our family, we've primarily stressed three rules.

* We don't hurt people.

* We don't hurt things.

* We don't hurt ourselves.

2. Don't threaten with unrealistic consequences.
"If you don't come here right now, Mommy's going to leave you." When you declare consequences that are not likely to happen, you teach an underlying belief that the child is above the law and can get

away with things. This will be problematic as s/he ages and conveys that attitude toward company policy and legal authorities. Obviously, there are times when a responsible parent will mandate immediate behavior, but this should be last resort versus the default. Select outcomes that are realistic to implement and then do so. Where possible, let natural consequences run their course. We mentioned this in Chapter 3 and noted how punishment tends to disempower leaders, while healthy discipline empowers them.

3. Provide options.

When you only give a young leader one choice, yours, you unnecessarily frustrate an innate drive leaders have to make decisions. Most leaders possess a noncompliance gene. When you say something can't be done, they intuitively feel motivated to prove it can. For example, instead of saying, "Quit playing your video game and go to bed," you might say, "You have two options. It's nine o' clock. Either you can go to bed now and play your video game after school tomorrow, or you can stay up until ten and not play your video the rest of the week. It's your choice." You haven't abdicated parenting because you've established parameters for the two options, but you provided a choice for your child. She will need to weigh the pros and cons, the outcomes, and then she will feel empowered to make the decision even if she may not enjoy the consequences either way. This is a challenge of leading. But your young leader feels esteemed by being offered a choice.

4. Use a graduated process for gaining desired behavior.

Young leaders frequently possess strong wills. In the appropriate place, this is a valuable strength. But adults who jump to the conclusion that a child is being intentionally disrespectful and rebellious will create unnecessary conflict. Consider a graduated approach that doesn't assume the worst.

A. Get the child's attention by speaking his name. Wait for a response, and then ask for the desired behavior. This ensures communication has really happened.

B. Make eye contact and repeat your request. Ask the child to repeat what you said, and then acknowledge that you value "first time obedience" or "first time cooperation."

C. If behavior is still unacceptable, ask, "Can you get yourself under control, or do you need my help?" This communicates seriousness but in an honoring manner that leaves them in control.

D. If this is ineffective, assume the child needs your assistance. Physically move him to comply, whether it is escorting him to a certain part of the room or helping him hold a ball that you asked him to stop bouncing.

E. As a last resort, remove him from the immediate environment and use this as a one-on-one opportunity to find out what's going on inside of him or talk "leadership" with him. Help him consider how his actions are impacting others and failing to reach the goal effectively.

This approach is generally effective from early childhood through preteens. After that, you need to respond as a boss or a superior because most teens possess the psyche of an adult even though they may not exhibit adult traits yet.

5. Use signals, not public embarrassment, to ask for attention or control.

If you have a young leader who consistently struggles with self-control, you may want to prearrange a communication system with her. Sometimes, adults try to embarrass young leaders in an attempt to belittle them publicly. This is the action of an adult who feels threatened and at a loss for more effective means. The problem is that while you may curtail their behavior temporarily, you're apt to damage the child's self-esteem and turn the influencer against you, causing further problems down the road.

Because leaders are good at influencing peers, they are prone to be sensitive to how they are treated in front of others. By nature, they are pied pipers. When you encounter an influencer with little self-discipline, it is helpful to pre-establish a "secret" code that communicates your need for the immature leader to exhibit more self-control, without public humiliation. This sign could be tugging at your ear lobe as you look at the child, a light tap on the shoulder as you walk past her, or some other cue that is discreet.

> **KidLead Idea:** *Think of a recent conflict in your family or with another child. How might you use the previous ideas to better respond to a similar situation next time?*

Steve Grant, adult leadership coach and KidLead Certified Trainer, on the importance of emotional intelligence and peer feedback

I really like Goleman's model on emotional intelligence (EI) that impacts a leader's performance and success. One of the things I found with my daughters is that they matured as leaders when they began to understand how their emotions were perceived by others (self-awareness) and how they impacted those around them positively and negatively. As a KidLead Trainer, it was obvious that some kids possess a large amount of EI, motivating them to be more inclusive, sensitive to those on the outer circle and those who were using manipulation to get results.

Another benefit is when we encourage peer feedback and teaching leaders to ask other participants how they might handle a project and how effectively they managed an exercise. The peer feedback is often more important to developing their leadership than adult feedback

---

Developing Problem Solving Skills

We teach KidLead Trainers and Koaches the importance of developing a decision making approach to coaching. Everyone needs problem solving skills in life, but a leader's ability to discover viable answers is crucial. Therefore, we want them to learn how to do this as effectively as possible while they're moldable. Unfortunately, in our attempt to be responsible adults, we accidently retard this development in young leaders. When faced with a challenge, problem, or difficult situation, there are four common responses. Only the fourth is apt to develop problem solving skills.

Power: Adults who feel out of control often resort to yelling, verbal put-downs, physical punishment, or asking rhetorical questions, such as, "When are you going to grow up?" and "Do you want a spanking?" When this happens frequently, a child typical becomes either aggressive or withdrawn. Eventually, s/he becomes immune to the responses so that the adult's power must increase to be noticed.

Suggesting: A second option adults choose, especially when a child mentions a concern, is trying to provide solutions for the child. Your daughter says, "My friends won't play with me." You respond, "Why don't you go swimming with Brooke, or why don't you invite Angie over to watch a movie?" While your intentions are good, the result is a child who remains passive, dependent on other's ideas, and who lacks creative problem solving skills.

Explaining: A third option adults take in helping a child resolve a problem is reasoning. "You won't have any friends if you do that." "Your teacher won't take that sassy mouth." The child eventually views this response as simply another mini-lecture and tunes it out. S/he doesn't change and feels detached from consequences.

Problem Solving: A fourth and effective approach is to engage a child in the problem solving process herself. This includes recognizing cognitive and emotional elements. The goal is to connect consequences with decisions. There are three aspects of a typical decision making situation worth exploring: feelings, solutions, and consequences.

- Explore Feelings

Begin by raising the level of awareness of those involved. Suppose your daughter hits her brother. You confront her by sitting down with her and asking, "How does hitting Benji make you feel?" "How do you think it makes your brother feel?" The goal is to consider consequences.

- Explore Solutions

After you unpack some of the emotions, you'll want to brainstorm alternatives. You might ask, "What do you think you could do next time your brother bugs you?" "Okay, what else?" The goal is to come up with a few possible responses, not just "the right one."

- Explore Consequences

Now you want to evaluate potential consequences of these options. "What do you think will happen if you hit your brother?" "What might help you remember not to hit your brother next time?" Like Dr. Phil asks, "How is it working for you?"

Josh Nelson, our middle son, tells a story of proactive problem solving as a young leader: "We belonged to an athletic club that had a tennis program. I felt frustrated that they were charging us junior players so much to play each other on Sunday afternoons. Therefore, I formed a group that I named FoCo (Fort Collins) Tennis and called about a dozen people I knew. We played at the high school courts. There was no charge, but everyone was required to bring a can of tennis balls to play. The club ended up shutting down their program because people pulled out when they realized they didn't have to pay to have an organized hit-around time."

We'll wrap up this chapter with some of the bullet points we provide in our KidLead certification and coach training. They represent some best practices and common errors we've noticed over the years.

Two Key Percents

Keep these dual amounts in mind as you coach:
- 75% of teaching is Socratic. Avoid telling. Your goal is to engage young leaders in discovery.
- 25% talking time is your maximum "air time" allowance. If you hear your own voice more than one fourth of the time, you're talking too much. Learn to give up control.

Socratic Teaching (Asking Strategic Questions):

Think of yourself as a tour guide more than a teacher. Learn to ask strategic questions:
1. Focus on the topic; avoid rabbit trail questions.
Ask: What is one thing you learned about leading from that activity?
Not: How did you enjoy that activity?

2. Consider options; don't just settle for one good answer.
Say: That's good. Let's think of four more ways we could have accomplished this.
Not: Wow, great answer. Okay, the next question is…

3. Look for teachable moments; great finds are found in failures.
Say: We lost the competition. What can we learn from that?
Not: Oh bummer, you didn't do well. We'll do better next time.

4. Avoid "yes/no" and rhetorical questions.
Ask: What are some ways we can do better next round?
Not: Do you think we can do better next time?

5. Focus on the activity more than the person.
Ask: If you were the leader, what might you have done differently?
Not: What could Josh do better next time?

6. Keep the feedback of people positive.
Ask: What's one thing Karli did well as the leader?
Not: What should Karli have done as the leader?

7. Convey value for leaders' opinions.
Ask: What do you think about how our team did in this activity?
Not: I think we did well, but we could have done better.

General Principles to Coach by:

- There are no wrong answers, but there may be more effective ones.

- Everyone deserves an opportunity to share; protect against time hogging.

- Help develop good listening skills, not just good answering skills.

- Reward desired behavior.

- Remember the mirror effect; kids reflect what they see in us.

Seven Mistakes of Ineffective Coaching:

- Telling/providing solutions/taking over.

- Failing to focus on the leader during activities.

- Talking too much.

- Allowing poor group dynamics.

- Lacking engagement; coach passivity.

- Lack of involvement among team members.

- Getting caught up in the competition yourself.

Positive, proactive coaching requires significant emotional intelligence from the adult. The benefit of consistently implementing this approach over time is a young leader who is thoughtful about problem solving, considers consequences, and is more effective in getting good results.

Scott Blanchard, son of leadership gurus Ken and Margie Blanchard, tells KidLead about how his dad disciplined him as a young leader.

Like many boys, I was not that interested in hearing other people's warnings or advice. I had the tendency of getting into mischief that grew over the years. One of the things that used to happen in my family, being raised by a leadership professor who was not yet guru status, along with my mom, who is a PhD, was how I was disciplined. I used to yearn to be punished like the kids down the street when they got into trouble, where they got restrictions, or grounded, or additional chores. My punishment involved sitting at the table and talking with my parents about how my behavior was incongruent with the stated family values.

What my parents would talk about is not what a kid wants to discuss. They'd ask, "What were you thinking? What results were you expecting from that action?" These conversations made me feel guilty, but what they were trying to do was to teach me to be more thoughtful about my actions. Their ideas and words had a lot of power on me as a young kid. The final blow was that my parents would ask, "What are you aiming for in life?"

I knew that if I didn't come up with a pretty good answer, I wasn't getting up from the table. So I'd say, "I want to go to Cornell University," where they went. Then I'd add, "I want to be successful, have a family, and take time in the summer like you do."

I knew that I had to answer their questions. After I did, my dad would say, "I'm glad you know where you're going. But if that's where you're going, look at your actions today. They are going in an entirely different direction. How are these choices going to get you where you want?"

That's the same question I ask leaders of companies today. If you're clear about your vision but your actions are taking you in a different direction, how are these actions taking you where you want to go? I ask my kids the same question. They are avid about their dreams, but as a father, I want to help them align their actions with where they want to go. There's value in thinking big and setting goals, but there's even more value in helping people take steps in those directions.

I'm amazed how many people have developed the idea that life is easy and success is a given, not requiring hard work. They don't think things through long-term and don't step up their daily activities to achieve them. The people successful in life understand the connection between hard and smart work and where they're going. My grandpa used to say that if you want to be successful in life, you only have to work half a day. You choose whether it's the first twelve hours or the second twelve hours.

Discussion Activators

1. What was the most helpful idea you got from this chapter?

2. Briefly describe a time when a parent or teacher blew it in the way s/he disciplined you. What can you learn from it when disciplining your children?

3. Positive parenting any child is important, but go deeper into why it can be more important for young leaders.

4. When is it important to be more parent than coach and vice versa?

Tell me, I forget.

Teach me, I might remember.

Involve me, I understand.

Chapter 7

Turning Home into a Leader Incubator

We teach that KidLead training programs are not substitutes for parents and guardians being involved with leadership development in a child's everyday life. The goal of our training is to "set the sail," but it's the parent's job to fill the sails. The benefit you have is creating and taking advantage of teachable moments on a regular and individualized basis. These become fertile soil to instill both values and skills that will become a part of the young leader's life for good. The difference between a parent growing a great grown-up and being a leader developer is that the latter establishes leadership situations.

Three Basic Ingredients Needed to Constitute a "Leadership" Situation:

1. There needs to be at least two other people involved on the "team."

Great life skills are numerous, but leading is about helping others achieve together. Being in charge of one person is okay, but there are far more dynamics for learning leadership when you have a minimum of three. If you're a single parent at home with an only child, you'll need to include cousins, friends, or others to expand the team.

2. There needs to be a measurable goal.

What is expected? Measuring outcomes is important, but be sure that the objective involves setting direction, organizing and/or accomplishing it in a new way. Even if it's a task as routine as team cleaning the house, you may suggest coming up with a new and more effective way of doing it.

3. There needs to be legitimate authority.

Although you're ultimately responsible as the parent, your young leader needs to know that s/he has a certain amount of authority to determine how to accomplish the task. This is room to spread his or her wings. Try to be clear *what* it is you'd like your young leader to do, not necessarily describing *how* to accomplish the task. While this increases the risk of failure, it enhances the child's sense of accomplishment and empowerment. Being in charge creates confidence. It's not just a play on words that "managing is different from leading." Merely having your child follow the directions that you provide is not authentic leading. Give your young leader sufficient room to do something new; don't just perpetuate what already exists. Responsibility without authority results in frustration. As a child progresses, you'll want to increase his or her authority as s/he demonstrates responsibility.

Leader Cues

Young leaders in **Lead**Now and **Lead**Well receive cue cards with the following ideas to use when it's their turn to be in charge of an activity. This is especially good for younger and less experienced leaders who may lack confidence or an awareness of keeping the leadership process moving. The main point is to spell the word: LEAD.

Listen to your team's ideas
"Our goal is to… So what are your ideas?"
"All right, what other ideas are there?"
"Thanks for sharing. Now let's get a plan."

Establish the plan
Select the ideas that seem the best.
"Here's the direction I think we should take…"
"This is how we'll get this done…"

Assign tasks
"Who wants to do what?"
"Ashley, we need you to..."
"Jesse, could you…?"

Determine the progress
If things are going well:
"Hey, nice job, team!"
"Great work, (name a team member)."
If things could go better:
"Let's work faster. Time is running out."
"Wait a second. Let's rethink our plan."

Feedfront and Feedback

If your child is young or lacks leading experience, you'll want to brainstorm ideas for accomplishing a task. This is what we call *feedfront*. One thing we've learned in training kids who are on the bubble or who may lack confidence in a leader role is to provide a few ideas from which s/he can choose. If possible, check in during the task to see how things are going, and troubleshoot.

"Mom, Sara's not setting the table like I asked."

"Okay, Jesse, why isn't she doing this? What would be some ways to motivate her to do this, instead of screaming at her?"

Most importantly, debrief after the project. Feedback questions are very important to the learning process, but they often get overlooked because we don't make time for them and they can feel anticlimactic to the activity. "What went well? What didn't go well? What could you do next time to be more effective?" Avoid scolding or punishing. Keep the questions neutral and matter-of-fact, and be very affirming. Treat your young leader the way you'd like to be treated as an adult in the workplace.

Four "getting going," "feedfront" coaching questions to ask:

1. What is it that you want to accomplish?

2. What are you going to need, and what do you have?

3. Whom are you going to select, and what strengths do they bring?

4. What are some ideas of how you can lead your team?

Four mid-course coaching questions to ask:

1. How is your team doing in accomplishing its tasks?

2. What could you change to be more effective?

3. What can you do to help your team work together?

4. How are you staying focused on the team and not doing the task yourself?*

*This last question is important among young leaders, who often get sucked into doing the activity themselves and lose sight of how their team is functioning. Chances are you'll need to bring this up consistently so that leaders understand the difference between team leading and team participating. While leaders can perform a function, they must always keep an eye on the overall performance of the team.

Four key feedback questions to ask after a leadership activity:

1. What did you do well as a leader, and what did your team do well?

2. What problems emerged, and how did you respond to them?

3. What is one thing you learned about leading from this project?

4. What is one thing you could do next time that might make your team more effective?

Four key feedback questions to ask team members after an activity, while remaining sensitive to the self-esteem of the leader:

1. How did the team do in working together?

2. Did we have the right people doing the right things? If not, what could we have done differently?

3. What did the leader do that was helpful?

4. If you were leading next time, what is one thing you may have done differently?

John Maxwell, bestselling author and
leadership expert, tells KidLead about a leadership
training idea he's used.

You can never start too young in teaching a child to lead. My dad
was profoundly influential in the leadership development of my brother
and myself. He not only modeled exceptional leadership, but he knew
how to invest in us individually to bring out what we needed.

One thing Dad did was something that I have done with our two
children: paying us to read good books on leaders. The key is rewarding
desired behavior. Paying your children to take out the trash is great if
you want them to become a garbage collector. Paying them to make
their bed or keep their rooms straight is okay if you want to raise a
maid. But pay them to read a good book, perhaps a biography on a
famous leader, and then have them tell you about it or write a report on
it. That way, they learn about these people and what made them great
leaders.

Leadership Projects

Most of the time, a few good ideas are all parents need to get
going. The following is a list of projects and task ideas that you can
implement in and around the home to help you grow great leaders.
A parent will have to use his or her best judgment in knowing how
much assistance to provide in terms of coaching. You want to help
young leaders get some early wins, but you also don't want to create
a dependent relationship. Plus, we often learn more from our failures,
so letting a young leader experience a setback here and there can be
a great learning opportunity if it is handled well.

Please send us your ideas that worked, and we'll try to share with
other parents and guardians through the KidLead website (**www.
kidlead.com**). Send your ideas to info@kidlead.com.

Meal Supervision

Don't just say, "You're in charge of getting dinner ready." Give your
young leader instructions for meal prep, including the following:

- You decide what we're going to eat.
- Do we have the right ingredients? If not, how will you go about making sure we do?
- When will we be eating? You'll need to check everyone's schedule.
- Where will we eat?
- Who's in charge of cooking?
- Who's setting the table?
- Who's in charge of cleanup?
- Determine who is going to be involved in the process: "the team"
- Who will do what, how, and by when?
- Debrief:
  - How did the team do in working together?
  - Were the right people doing the right things?
  - What did the leader do that was helpful?
  - What could the leader do next time to be more effective?

Garage/Room Cleaning Supervision

Instead of saying, "Clean up the garage," give your young leader instructions for cleaning or rearranging the garage in a way that includes the following:

- Who is going to be involved on the team?
- What needs to be accomplished?
- Do you have the needed resources to do this (e.g., garbage bags, paint, shelving, etc.)?
- When does this need to be accomplished?
- What is the plan for accomplishing this?
  - Who's going to do what, when, how?
  - Who is the best at doing what?
  - How will you determine quality?

Debrief:
  - How did the team do in working together?
  - Were the right people doing the right things?
  - What did the leader do that was helpful?
  - What could the leader do next time to be more effective?

Landscape Supervision

Instead of saying, "Clean up the yard, pull the weeds, mow the lawn, or rake the leaves," give your young leader instructions for landscaping by asking:

- What needs to be accomplished?
- Do you have the necessary tools and resources? If not, how will you obtain these?
- Who is going to be involved on the team?
- Who's good at what?
- When does this need to be accomplished?
- Debrief:
  - How did the team do in working together?
  - Were the right people doing the right things?
  - What did the leader do that was helpful?
  - What could the leader do next time to be more effective?

Trip Planning

If you're planning a day off or weekend getaway, don't just tell the kids what you're going to do, put them in charge. Give your young leader instructions by asking:

- What are we going to do on the trip?
  - Who needs to give an opinion?
  - How will you negotiate different opinions?
  - What if someone can't go? How will you determine whether to go or not?
- How long will it take?
- How far away is it?
- Who's involved in the process, and what abilities do they have (e.g., driving)?
- What will this cost?
  - Who'll pay for it?
  - Is this in the budget?
- What do we need to take on this trip?
- Who will determine the map and/or get directions?

- How will we know if this was a good trip or not?
- Is there anything else we need to do (e.g., take care of a pet, pack bags, bring food or drink, buy tickets, arrange a babysitter, etc.)?
- Debrief:
  o How did the team do in working together?
  o Were the right people doing the right things?
  o What did the leader do that was helpful?
  o What could the leader do next time to be more effective?

Josh Nelson on leading and responsibility

On thing I liked about the way my parents raised us is that they gave us responsibility, starting small and then giving us more and more. For example, if they told us to be home by 10:00 p.m., and we were, then next time they'd give us more freedom. I think this relates to leadership in that leadership doesn't happen without responsibility. If you don't learn responsibility, then there's not as good of a chance that you'll be able to lead.

Adopt A Family

Whether it's the holidays or anytime of year, why not let your young leader organize the family and others to gather funds, supplies, presents, and goodies for a family struck with poverty, a struggling single parent, or an aging couple? Consider house cleaning, yard work, gifts, childcare, or any number of other ideas to provide support and care for a family in need.

Care Scheduling

When someone is having a health crisis or can use an extra hand during some other type of life trauma, offer extra help for childcare, meals, lawn care, or other support issues. Encourage your young leader to find out what could help the person, develop a plan and a strategy, and recruit a team to accomplish the task. One of the biggest challenges is finding and scheduling others to help. This responsibility could teach your young leader the *task of ask*, a lifelong skill leaders must develop to be effective. Then helping volunteers follow through is a different challenge. Let's say the next-door neighbor just had hip surgery. A young leader could contact the person to see what might be helpful. "Dinner would be great the next two weeks," the neighbor says. The child can then coordinate with family, friends, faith community members, and neighbors to schedule bringing daily meals to the recovering person.

Choir Leading

If your child has musical ability, consider helping him or her arrange to become a children's choir leader. Consider a preschool group at a church or childcare facility. The organizational activities, such as getting music, scheduling rehearsal times, and working with adult assistants, help young influencers learn how to lead. Then, when it's time to perform, consider elements of marketing, event planning (i.e., refreshments, programs, greeters) and recruiting assistants. The young leader can grasp a big picture of the various elements that go into a single project. While leading a children's choir as an adult may be more of a teaching skill, as a preteen or teen, it takes on a greater dynamic of leading younger peers, working with adults, and building confidence with groups of people.

Coach Kids' Sports Team

If your young leader has athletic ability and passion for a certain sport, consider how you might assist him or her to become a coach or assistant coach of an athletic team. Community athletic groups are often looking for coaches. For example, say your child is a little leaguer or avid baseball fan. What about allowing him or her to coach a T-ball team? Talk to the T-ball coordinator or a T-ball coach and discuss the idea. So long as there is appropriate adult supervision, leading younger kids is a great opportunity to exercise leadership. Most groups will have an age limit for coaches, but there's no reason why you or another adult can't be the official coach while allowing the young leader ample opportunity to get experience coaching younger kids.

Joe Lawrence, leadership trainer, www.InspireTomorrow. com, shares a leader story from his childhood.

When I was thirteen years old, I was thrown into a leadership role with over sixty people, and I got hooked on leading. I've been in martial arts since the age of eight. I quit a few times and returned at twelve. A year later, I was well on my way toward earning my black belt. One day, one of the Black Belts that led the class could not make it, so the instructor decided to test me. He had me lead the entire class for two hours. About twenty people in the class actually outranked me. At first I was honored to get this opportunity. "Wow, all these people are doing what I say." Being thrown into a leadership situation can be scary, but it's also a place to shine.

Family Budget Plans

Consider going over the family income, bills, and wish list for a month. Let the child know what it will cost to "run" the family. Then let the child call a family meeting to discuss how everyone can best work within the budget, what needs or wants should take priority, and what should be postponed until the next pay period. In addition to learning lessons about income, expenses, and responsibility, your child will learn the process of negotiating priorities with limited resources.

Fundraising

Local charities are often in need of extra funds. Think of a potential community service topic that your young leader is passionate about, whether it's animals, the homeless, poor people, or those who are physically challenged. Find a local charity that aids this cause. Let your young leader brainstorm ways of raising awareness and/or funds or needs for this agency. It may be something like organizing a car wash, going door-to-door for canned goods, or doing garage sales of gathered items from friends and neighbors. Consider letting the local media know, in hopes of bringing awareness of this agency as well as inspiring others to donate time and money. (Send news clips to info@KidLead.com.)

Game in a Bottle

The Game in a Bottle activity is similar to some of the accelerated learning activities we use in KidLead training modules, but it can be a fun thing to do at home. Most of us have a game in a box that we have outgrown or never use that takes up space in a closet. You can also pick up a one or two dollar game at a garage sale or thrift store. Get an empty 2-liter plastic soft drink bottle and put it next to the box game. Gather the family or your young leader's friends. Ask your child to be in charge of the team to accomplish this outlandish task: "Your challenge is to get the box game into the 2-liter bottle. Everything must be in it, but you can't tear or cut the bottle." Most normal-sized box games can fit. You can add some dynamics by giving them a time limit, such as thirty minutes.

Garden Planting

Let your young leader supervise the family garden. This activity includes an array of tasks. These include obtaining resources and developing a budget for plants, tools, and supplies. Plus, there is research regarding soil types, moisture, growing periods, need for sunlight, fertilizing, and other horticultural details. Remember, for it to be truly leadership, there needs to be a team to coordinate for accomplishing these varied tasks. Don't worry about having a few plants that don't grow, because we learn more from our failures than our successes.

Gift Wrapping

Don't miss an opportunity to teach leadership to a child and get some chores done at the same time. Naturally, you won't want family members wrapping their own gifts, but let your young leader work on a plan to lead the family in gift wrapping. Tasks can include gathering supplies, scheduling within busy holiday schedules, making a check-off list, and perhaps even doing some training and quality assurance.

Team Shop

Whether it's going back to school or grocery shopping, consider encouraging your young leader to get some friends together who have a set budget, and then plan how to best use their money. This may involve some preliminary cost research, determining the best stores, and then shopping as a group while discussing opinions, making decisions, and accomplishing the task in a certain amount of time. Returns are a part of shopping, so teach responsibility by putting them in charge of taking items back in case a purchase isn't quite right.

Internet Biz

Your young leader is probably familiar with the World Wide Web, sending e-mails, and other computer skills. Why not help your child develop a website that would involve others so that s/he can develop leadership skills of recruiting, motivating, and casting vision? For a nominal fee, sometimes included in your current Internet service, you can have a website that can be created with user-friendly software. Perhaps it's a weekly e-news service for kids, letting them know what's going on in your community for families and kids. Maybe it's a "Dear Abby" advice column for selecting school attire, getting along with parents or siblings, or even a tutorial on some sort of skills. Perhaps it's covering news of a youth sports team or league. Your kids can determine if they want to sell ads or get sponsors. Dream up ideas.

Leaf Raking Biz

Raking leaves is a great young leader business in parts of the country where leaves fall. Like all of these ideas, getting others to be a part of the team will turn it from an individual work opportunity to a leadership learning one. Who'll be on the team? Who'll do what? What will we charge? What tools will we need? Where will we get the tools? Where will we dispose of the leaves? How will we market the biz? What will the team members be paid? Who'll schedule the work?

Paper Route with a Twist

There are not a lot of opportunities for kids to find employment before the age of sixteen. A paper route is one. But just having a paper route is not necessarily a leadership process, even though it builds confidence, teaches responsibility, and nurtures a work ethic, all great assets to leading. If you give it a twist, it can become a leadership process. What if your KidLeader hires other kids who'll do some of the work? As "subcontractors," the other kids become team members whom your young leader will need to recruit, negotiate pay rates, motivate, schedule, and train. When team members have to go on vacations or quit, these real life lessons prepare your young leader for similar situations in adult life.

Party Planning

Encourage your young leader to plan a party that will be run by a small team of people. A variety of things will need to be considered, such as adult supervision, theme, food, timing, location, resources, preparation, cleanup, and communication. Take a backseat as you let the children run this event for their peers or other families.

Pet Care Biz

People are always looking for someone who can provide care for their pets, whether it's watering, feeding, and walking pets while the owners are away, or merely cleaning up poop in the yard. But doing this alone is not a leadership situation, even though children can develop good qualities from this. But if your child "hires" others to be a part of this team and recruits them to work, get new business, market, and be scheduled to cover the responsibilities of commitments made, then you have a leadership learning opportunity.

Jesse Nelson (at age fourteen)

I really like the way my parents raised me and taught me about leadership. But one thing I think they could have improved on was to help me learn about leadership even younger than they did. I think that a lot of times, kids are in the background of things instead of being allowed to make decisions and lead.

Restroom Cleaning Biz

Who hasn't had a bad restroom experience in a local gas station or small business? What if your young leader started a restroom cleaning service that provided daily care for local facilities needing refreshment? Recruiting staff members would make it a leadership opportunity, involving scheduling, managing materials purchases, negotiating pay, motivating, arranging transportation, handling conflict, and training. (Of course, getting your leader to start with his own bathroom would be good.)

Snow Removal Biz

If you live in cold country, chances are there will be opportunities for your young leader to develop a team of people who'll remove snow, either for free for people in need, or for a fee for the rest of us. Recruiting team members, gathering resources (shovels, snow blowers, bags of salt, adequate clothing) advertising, setting fees, scheduling work, and handling all that goes into activating a team will help your child learn valuable leadership skills and gain invaluable experience.

Vacant Lot Cleanup

Ever notice how certain lots seem to collect garbage, junk, and litter? What if you encouraged your young leader to recruit a team of people to clean up the site? Obviously, you'd want to check safety issues (toxic waste, local guard dogs, or unfriendly owners), but what a great opportunity to spruce up the community as your child learns philanthropy, team building, resource procurement (trash bags, gloves, refreshments, disposal), and responsibility.

Mario Soberal, leadership trainer, shares a story on taking his son to work.

Years ago when my children were young, I would take them into the office, and they would spend the day with me. The thing that was most important was that they learned how to deal with issues that arose by watching how I responded. Jake (10) was sort of bugging me when I needed to focus, so I gave him a pad of paper and told him to talk to the team and figure out what they needed to do a better job. He came back with a long list. I asked him what made the most sense, and he picked out one item in particular. A gal named Judy said she'd be more effective in sales if she had a window view, where she could clear her mind periodically.

A few months later, Jake was back in the office. I gave him a pad and told him to walk around again and see what people needed. He chanced by Judy's cube, who we'd been able to get a window view. "How do you like your cube?" Jake asked. "I really had to work hard to sell my dad on it, but he realized it was a great idea." Judy laughed. Jake is now in his second year of law school and wants to be President of the United States some day. The more kids are exposed to leadership roles, the more they see the possibilities around them.

Discussion Activators

1. What are three ideas you could readily implement in your family situation?

2. What are the unique challenges you may need to overcome in your family situation to provide leadership opportunities for your child (e.g., single home, only child, empty-nesters, special needs siblings, etc.)?

The only real training for leadership

is leadership.

-Anthony Jay

Chapter 8

Creating Leader-Friendly Classrooms

Josh Nelson shares a classroom experience

I think that a lot of times, kids get in trouble for disrupting the peace and rebuked for sticking out. They get rewarded for blending in, but leaders often don't do that. I remember one time in second grade, I didn't agree that a girl in class was allowed to skip watching several Spanish instructional videos. Some of the other kids felt the same way. I got in trouble because I talked to the teacher in front of everyone, stating that we didn't think this was fair. You might say it was a small revolt. I represented a group of us that felt this was not right because she was getting preferential treatment by the teacher.

The teacher asked me to stay after class. She told me that I showed leadership in the classroom, but I needed to "get along better with my classmates."

Leader-Aversive Classroom Culture

Scenarios like Josh's (above) go on daily in classrooms across America. I highly admire the heart and hard work of most school teachers and administrators I've met over the years. At the same time, the typical classroom culture is leader aversive. The teacher's desire for compliance, given a class of twenty to thirty students, makes it difficult for the budding and often non-compliant leader to constructively develop his or her gifts. Few teachers receive specific training on effectively handling students with leadership aptitude. Just as a nail sticking out of a floor is apt to get pounded down, young leaders experimenting with their influence abilities are more often reprimanded than rewarded by well-meaning educators seeking control of the classroom.

Certainly exceptions exist, and we applaud those professionals who recognize not only academic gifting but social aptitudes that deserve unique attention. While student leaders tend to be intelligent and good pupils, early bloomers are often not exceptional. Teachers commonly mistake academic success for leadership ability. We've found that isn't necessarily true. Gifted and Talented (GT) students are often confused as leaders and placed on student council. Sometimes those with high IQs lack social skills that win the respect of peers. This awkwardness is often overlooked in arenas that reward good grades and academic smarts. A running joke in colleges reflects this principle: "Professors, be nice to your 'A' students because they'll come back as fellow professors. But be really nice to your 'C' students because they'll return to endow your program."

One of KidLead's goals is to elevate the education and training of those who work with young leaders, including teachers. With a little tweaking, most teachers can significantly improve the leadership development in their classes. The following are ten practical suggestions for creating a leader-friendly classroom. This is also a self-serving strategy because when you begin harnessing the natural gifting of certain students, they will help you run the class and become positive allies. Miss these opportunities and you'll forever be battling troublemakers. From the classrooms I've observed as a parent and substitute teacher, I'm convinced that a significant number of disruptions could be reduced by creating a leader-friendly classroom and redirecting the influence of young leaders.

Ten Ways to Create Leader-Friendly Classrooms

1. Identify the top two to five influencers.

These are the kids who, when they crack a joke or make a comment, turn heads. The Pareto Principle, also known as the 80/20 rule, can be applied socially. Less than 20 percent of a student body will significantly influence the remaining 80 percent. In a typical class of thirty, you're apt to have two to five who demonstrate a natural aptitude for leading. Notice which kids are more popular, express opinions, and are followed in class, at lunch, and on the playground. The big difference between popularity alone and leadership is that leaders organize and direct, whereas popularity alone lacks these two qualities. One exception is the well-behaved, initially quiet leader who is waiting to be tapped on the shoulder for an opportunity to lead. Lacking confidence, these students are still respected by their peers.

Tiffany Miller, elementary teacher and KidLead Certified Trainer

As a teacher, I see how few leadership skills many students demonstrate. Everyday I try to find those kids whom I can help target their inner leadership ability. Not every child in my room can control a group or make the tough decisions, but I do have a few. These are the kids who draw the other students. When asked to move desks, these are the students who volunteer to create the seating chart. I asked the class to vote on two people to be the "leaders." These leaders would then guide the discussion and make sure the class was incorporated into the new desk arrangement. One boy led the discussion and made sure that not only the class agreed but that the seating arrangement worked for everyone. This entire idea was based upon one student's vision to create unity and leadership in the class. This by far is the best part of my job, developing their leadership potential.

2. Seek input from parents/guardians.

If you're unsure about a child's influence aptitude, check your hunches by interviewing parents about how their child acts in extracurricular activities, at home, and in the neighborhood. This will likely confirm your suspicions. Let them know you've identified their child as a leader so that you can team up to develop him or her. It's also a positive way to gain allegiance if and when you need to have a friendly chat regarding any class disruptions.

3. Specifically invest in a relationship with influencers.

While we all enjoy being liked, taking the time to know the habits, hobbies, interests, and activities of your identified leaders will go a long way in creating an ally relationship, especially when you need to ask a favor or confront an attitude. Although this may appear to be preferential treatment, we know that in any given classroom, each student is not given equal time anyway. The key is how and when you do this. Figure out how you can establish rapport. This improves your efficacy in confronting unacceptable behaviors if they occur. When teachers fail to gain the respect of young leaders, critique and discipline are less likely to be responded to positively. Playing the authority card ("Because I say so.") is less effective with leaders than others.

4. Intentionally create a positive role for young leaders.

Some teachers make the mistake of putting leaders in charge of watch-dogging their peers. Preteens we've talked to don't like this because it tends to place them in awkward positions of using their natural strengths in ways that alienate them from their peers, a.k.a. social suicide. Instead, make up activities or titles for kids with influence skills that seek to use their abilities more positively. Give these students special responsibilities, whether it's running errands, monitoring a class when you need to step out, or being team leaders for group activities. Not only are you helping them develop their gifts; you are also gaining allies.

5. Develop after school projects that tap leading, not just individual helping.

This may give you more options if your in-class opportunities are limited and/or there is a class rotation, as in middle schools. Whether it's cleaning the room, removing bulletin board décor, or rearranging the desks and chairs, consider added responsibilities. When possible, don't just use the leader alone, but let him or her direct a group of peers to do projects. Adults may fear this sort of structure will create resentment among kids not selected. Yet most children will have little conscious awareness of this practice because they already recognize these kids as peer leaders. This assumes that the teacher has effectively selected those gifted in leading. Let these young leaders practice their skills. Be creative. Gather them to brainstorm possible projects in and around the classroom. If you see others expressing leadership behaviors, feel free to provide opportunities for them as well to discover their talents.

KidLead Idea: *If you're a teacher or a parent activist for your school, pause a moment to respond to the 5 previous ideas by writing down ways to implement these in the classroom.*

6. Once a month, have lunch in your room with your young leaders.

This can be an opportunity for you to get to know them better, ask for suggestions, and brainstorm ways to make the class better. Leaders like to share their ideas and feel respected when given a chance to do so. You can make up a name for this group. The benefit is that leaders recognize each other. Even though these students may not be friends naturally, they will learn to respect each other. Since each influencer will have unique spheres of influence, this gives you greater coverage of the entire class. Relax and make it fun.

When you gather ideas, it's helpful if you can actually implement some so the students can see that you value their input. Josh Nelson reported an example of this in one of his college classes.

The professor had recruited an assistant teacher who proctored an exam. Some of the students were cheating by using their textbooks. When the professor heard that, the next day he asked how he could make it right. He said he wanted one student to talk to him on behalf of the class to do what they thought was right. I stood up and said that those who didn't use their books should be rewarded for doing the honorable thing. After I spoke, others stood and shared their ideas. The teacher took some of my suggestions and said he'd try to determine who didn't use their texts and would try to make it right with the class.

7. Talk to the principal and other teachers for leadership projects.

You may not have enough project ideas to develop the leaders you've identified in your classroom. Another idea is to talk to your colleagues about projects they might have. You could also talk to your principal, custodians, and lunchroom staff. Perhaps there's a neighboring vacant lot that needs cleaning. A school principal can do a lot to elevate the value of raising leaders throughout the school. Teachers who buy into the importance of leadership development can share ideas with each other. This is especially beneficial as students graduate from one grade to the next, when leadership-oriented teachers inherit young leaders who've been developed in the classroom of a colleague.

> **KidLead Idea:** *(Provided by Tiffany Miller, elementary school teacher and KidLead Trainer)*
>
> *I like to start the year with 'paradigm shifts.' This allows students to take leadership roles and create a bond with others. This also allows me to see who steps up to the plate and who the leaders are in my room. I do a few activities that allow the kids to 'take over.' For example, I do a paradigm shift in science class to reveal you can think outside the box. The students are instructed to create a flying craft using only a piece of paper and paperclip. The goal is to hit a paper target. The inner ring is worth 5 points and the outer 1. If they miss the entire target, it's 0. Most kids assume that the craft is to be an airplane, similar to ones they have made in the past. I let them decide how groups should be formed.*
>
> *After each takes a turn to hit the target from about 5 feet away, they get another 10 minutes to discuss their new plan. This is when leadership usually emerges. The leader usually selects the student whose craft hit the target, reconstructing that same one. Sometimes a kid will ask if it has to be an airplane. The leader is the facilitator. The only rule is to use the materials you have and be 5 feet away. Then a few create balls of paper and call them their 'aircraft.' This demonstrates teamwork and a paradigm shift. I use activities like these throughout the year so they learn to push the envelope and be creative in groups.*

8. Move influencers away from the windows and doors.

These are places of distraction. When a leader is distracted, others pull away emotionally. If possible, keep the influencers closer to your desk so they feel more a part of the action and your authority. You can make eye contact with influencers and tap their shoulder as you walk past your desk. If you've created rapport with them, spread them around the room so that they serve as informal area influencers.

9. Connect influencers with mentors and community leaders.

Invite adult leaders to interact with you and your identified leaders, whether it's at lunch or after school. This might involve a field trip with parents. Tap the potential of others who can *speak into the lives* of these future influencers. By creating a simple mini-extracurricular program, you intensify your bonding with these young leaders. Plus, you position yourself as a teacher who understands the importance of mentoring and leadership development, raising your value as a teacher among parents and administrators. Consider a leadership club that maximizes these introductions. Do not underestimate a community leader's willingness to go out of her way to interact with your leaders, so long as you convey the uniqueness of your group. Leaders tend to relate to and enjoy each other regardless of age.

10. Work hard at disciplining and not punishing your class leaders.

Although we've addressed this in the previous chapter, it's worth repeating again in the context of the classroom. While it's tempting to intimidate or embarrass young leaders who are resisting your authority, work hard not to dishonor them. They have a sense that their peers respect them, so when an authority figure tries to diminish them publicly, it will often backfire. Sending them to the principal's office, interrupting class to verbally flog them, or bringing significant attention to their failure will create an emotional barrier to you that you can't afford. While compliants will quickly respond to correction, non-compliants are apt to become passive-aggressive or aggressive. Either one is detrimental to classroom harmony and productivity.

> **KidLead Idea:** *Pause to respond to ideas 6 through 10 by writing ways to implement these ideas in the classroom if you're a teacher or a parent activist for your school.*

We all have memories of teachers who made an impact in our lives. That's why many educators entered the field—to make a difference in lives. But when you change the life of a future leader, your influence has multiple effects. Since most leaders are not recognized as such or developed until adulthood, the chances significantly increase that you'll be long remembered when you see the potential in them as students. To make this difference when leaders are moldable is to leave your mark on all whom that leader will eventually influence as well.

Stephen Arterburn, founder of New Life Treatment Centers, tells KidLead about his family leadership experiences.

I had the privilege of having a dad who said he was proud of me. He'd always find something to brag about me, even when I was crummy at something. I was telling my daughter this and she said, "Well of course. You must be the most productive person, next to Johnny Depp." My dad believed I could be a leader but didn't make me feel like I had to be like him. The world was my limit. I have Attention Deficit Disorder, but I wanted to make a difference. That's what he instilled in me.

He also showed me servanthood. I have two stepsons, ages seven and nine. I told them how my dad, every Christmas, would buy groceries and take us to the poor side of town. We'd go to a home where there was a room lined with people and a single light bulb hanging in the middle. We'd deliver food and gifts. When I told my boys this story, they said, "Let's do that!" So we went to Walgreens and bought gift cards. The boys wrote on the envelope, "From God and a family who loves you." We went downtown and passed out the gift cards. We'd see a guy riding a bike in thirty-degree weather and we'd give him one. We saw a pregnant woman and five men going into a Rescue Mission and we gave each of them a gift card. My five-year-old said, "Man, this is great!"

Setting an example of giving is the best thing you can do. Leading isn't taking all the good stuff, but giving what you've got and hoping that other people will come around you and follow your lead. Too many leaders feel entitled, but that's not what leading is about. It becomes their downfall or their greatest limitation.

Discussion Activators

1. What was the most helpful idea you got from this chapter?

2. Share a story from your school experience as a child or youth where a teacher enhanced or diminished your leadership ability.

3. If you are a teacher, consider two to three "next steps" you can do in a week or two to create a leader-friendly classroom. If you're not a teacher, how can you become a child- leader advocate in your school?

Don't judge each day by the harvest you reap,

but by the seeds you plant.

–Robert Louis Stevenson

Chapter 9

Finding a Leader-Mentor for Your Child

You Can Do It

In ancient times, as in many cultures today, the village setting allowed people to help raise each others' children. When tribal elders invested in young leaders, it created an organic strategy for perpetuating influencers. That's all but lost in America. According to Peter Drucker, known as the father of modern management, local communities of faith are the closest setting to this remaining in our culture. As a result of losing the village effect, we lack natural mentoring, where informal, non-parent contact is individualized. Mentoring is beneficial for all kids, but it is vital in growing a great leader.

Even though there is a touch of mentoring that we have designed into our KidLead training programs, where the trainer and Koaches provide individualized attention to young leaders, we highly encourage parents to seek additional mentoring opportunities. This allows children to interact with leaders in the community, who can leave a positive mark on a young leader's life. A mentor is different from a trainer, teacher, or coach. A mentor is a person who invests in a person individually, passing on life experience and wisdom.

Most of us feel a bit intimidated when we think of finding or being a mentor. Perhaps it's because we see influencing a young person other than our children as such an awesome responsibility. Maybe it's because we don't feel worthy or that we're just plain embarrassed to ask or be asked. More than likely, few of us have experienced a mentoring relationship, so replicating it doesn't come natural. Then there's the social awkwardness created by unfortunate cases of child abuse and molestation, causing responsible people to feel paranoid about a one-on-one connection with a minor.

But more than anything, the reason we don't mentor or pursue mentoring relationships for our children is that we're not sure what to do. We've made it out to be a big commitment spanning long periods of time, akin to a corporate internship or foster parenting. But this need not be. You can make a big impact in a short time with a little effort that young leaders will remember for years to come.

Short-term mentoring impacts a young life for two reasons. First, the one-on-one interest of another adult in the life of a young person makes a difference. Your presence communicates value, esteem, and belief in this future leader because it's not your job to do this. Secondly, adult experiences we take for granted, such as staff meetings, business calls, and any number of tasks related to our job as leaders, create a potent memory to a young leader whose life has pretty much been defined by entertaining media, family, school, sports, and peers. Don't underestimate the positive impact on a child sitting in your office, listening in as you call a client and watching your interactions with colleagues.

Our middle son, Josh, demonstrated a flair for business as a preteen. He'd ride his bicycle around our neighborhood, collecting "House for Sale" flyers, figuring out the cost per square footage and letting us know when there was a good deal or overpriced home. We're not business-oriented, so we asked a friend of ours who is an entrepreneur to let Josh hang out with him for a day or two, simply shadowing him and letting him ask questions. The man was checking out a rental property to invest in, so as they walked through the house, he asked Josh how much money he had. Josh told him, and the man asked, "How'd you like to go in 10 percent of a rental property?" "Sure," Josh said. So at the age of fourteen, Josh made his first real estate investment.

Awhile later, we arranged for Josh to talk to a friend who was a certified financial planner. The man ended up offering Josh a part-time job in his office, sending out checks and such. The man gave him a brief introduction to investing in stocks, and Josh ended up buying shares of a company as a fourteen-year-old. He's continued to monitor, buy, and sell stocks since. Josh, in turn, mentored Jesse (his younger brother), who became a stock owner at the age of twelve. While this type of mentoring is good for all kids, it illustrates opportunities around us to introduce our young leaders to people who lead in their work. They introduce expertise, experiences, styles, and insights beyond our own.

Mentoring is a powerful force in the life of a young leader. The following ideas show how to find a mentor for your young leader and how to serve as a mentor.

Finding a Mentor for Your Kid

- Consider a friend or family member who has an expertise different from yours. Obviously, you'll need to use your head regarding logistics, timing, and trust, but don't let these details deter you from asking someone to do a mentor meeting with your child. Most people feel honored to be asked. You may even want to avoid the term "mentor," as it can be intimidating. Use phrases such as "shadowing you," "watching you work," or "spending time with you at your job."
- Ask the mentor to meet one to two times with your child for one to two hours each time. This need not be a long or protracted arrangement. It works best if this is done in the mentor's office or workspace, as opposed to a neutral meeting place where the leader is out of his or her leading environment.
- Provide interaction suggestions (such as those in the following section). This reduces the mentor's anxiety and provides some simple coaching ideas that will help the "yes" come easier when you ask. You may also train your child to be mentored by supplying him or her with some good questions as well. (We'll provide some later in this chapter.)
- Suggest a schedule where your child can actually observe some leadership behaviors. There are a lot of things leaders do that aren't leading. They eat, drink, read e-mails, and do any number of other things that everyone does. When a potential mentor asks what to do, suggest tasks s/he does pertaining to his or her role as a leader. This may involve interacting with other people, making decisions, checking on a big project, and working with staff. The best suggestion may be to simply allow the young leader to shadow the mentor through a typical

half-day schedule. It may not seem exciting to the leader, but it will likely be pretty cool for the young leader. Provide room for talk time and unpacking a meeting or event.

- Thank the mentor, and then review the experience with your young leader. Talk about his or her experience and what the mentor said or did.

KidLead Idea: Make a list of people you know or work with who could spend an hour or two with your child.

Eight Mentoring Ideas

Here are some ideas you can use if you are asked to serve as a mentor or, better yet, if you initiate a mentoring meeting with a young influencer.

1. Talk to the child like an adult, a future leader.

Don't worry about "dumbing down" your conversation. Consider how you'd talk to a new friend or outsider who may not know about your industry or profession.

2. Tell the young leader what you do.

Provide a simple explanation of what your company does. Many of us do our work without thinking a lot about it, especially if we've been doing it for a while. Don't worry about trying to impress or entertain the young leader. Be yourself.

3. Describe how people function as teams.

How do you interact with them? What are the primary tasks of the teams and team members?

4. Show him or her your work environment.

This may involve attending meetings, visiting a job site, or taking a look at your office. If needed, introduce the young leader to others. This esteems the child. It also models your belief in mentoring and investing in future leaders to your team members and colleagues as they see you interacting with a protege.

5. Think of a problem you faced and how you attempted to solve it.

Don't worry about all the details, but simply explain a challenge to illustrate what you do. People looking from the outside rarely see the difficulties you face. Consider asking the protégé what s/he might have done in that situation.

6. Ask the young leader about his or her goals/aspirations.

By showing interest and asking questions, you're esteeming the young leader. Plus, you're discovering potential areas where their interests and what you do overlap.

7. Ask the young leader open-ended questions.

Instead of asking, "Did you think that was interesting?" ask, "What was something you thought was interesting during the meeting?"

8. Briefly tell the parent what you did and discussed so s/he can review the experience with the child.

If you enjoyed the time, you may offer to do it again. If not, then don't worry about extending an invitation, and don't feel badly about it either. Some kids will naturally resonate with you based on their age, personality, and interests. Others will not, but that's okay. You've done a good job by simply being available.

Bill Hybels, pastor of Willowcreek Community Church, one of the nation's largest congregations, tells KidLead how his dad developed his leadership ability.

When you're trying to develop leadership in young people, probably the most important single dynamic is to entrust them with unusual amounts of risk or responsibility at an early age. My father used to push me out on boats that were four or five times the size of the ones that I should have been able to handle. Then he'd say, "See you in a couple of hours." I was flying airplanes from the time I was twelve. When you do this, it teaches resourcefulness and humility. You think, "I'm going to have to ask questions because I don't know the way. I have to think of who can help me with this. That is a really good leadership trait. It also builds confidence.

I was thrown into so many situations so young, that by the time I was in my twenties and the idea came to start a church, for which I had no experience, I had the basic confidence in me that if I had some good people around me and took my time, I could sort it out. It was not unlike a hundred other things that I had to figure out along the way. So often I see young people who have a good education but have never been entrusted with risk or responsibility in large enough magnitude to have developed the kind of muscle that it takes to lead well.

Questions Young Leaders Can Ask Mentors

When a young leader has something prepared to talk about, it can help the child as well as the mentor. One idea is to write questions on a sheet of paper and place them in a notebook for your child to reference. S/he can also use the paper to take notes. This can reduce awkward moments of silence when either person is wondering what to say next. When you explain this to your child, you may want to encourage note taking. This improves attentiveness and provides you with information for a debrief or even a simple report. This can also serve as a neat memento for years to come if the person is famous or influential in his or her field. The following is a list of possible questions. We suggest selecting no more than ten, depending on the type of mentor and meeting and so as not to overwhelm either person with too many questions.

- What do you do in your work?
- How did you get into your career?
- When you were young, when did you realize what you wanted to do?
- What do you like about your job? What do you not like?
- Who was influential in your life when you were young and why?
- What are some goals you are trying to achieve?
- How do you help people work together to accomplish these goals?
- Can you explain a recent example of this?
- How do you try to solve problems?
- What have you learned about leadership over the years?

- How would you describe your leadership style?
- What are your strengths?
- What is one mistake you've made, and what did you learn from it?
- What advice would you give me as a young leader?
- As you look at the future, what opportunities do you see?
- As you look at the future, what problems do you see?
- What's one thing you'd still like to accomplish in life?
- If you could change one thing about your work, what would it be?
- What would you recommend I read?
- What would you recommend I do to improve my leadership?

> **KidLead Idea:** *Consider doing a swap where you mentor a friend's child and s/he mentors yours. Another option is to accompany your child, but note that this is for the child, not you. Don't dominate conversations with the mentor or attempt to rescue the child (or mentor) in quiet moments.*

Mentoring is a powerful tool that parents can use to develop their young leaders. Establishing a meaningful mentoring experience is not difficult. It's a high return on investment.

Discussion Activators

1. Name a person in your life who was a mentor or who influenced you in a way that made a positive mark in your life.

2. Mentoring is relational more than informational, meaning that it doesn't just dispense knowledge; it puts people together. Why do you think mentoring is given so little emphasis in our culture?

The better the start,

the stronger the finish.

Chapter 10

Leading Up and Laterally

Redefining "Politics"

You'll often hear adults refer to "office politics," the gamesmanship that happens when people leverage relationships to get their way. While kids don't use the term, they are all too familiar with the schoolyard version. While the word "political" usually has a negative connotation—as in "He's very political," implying he's conniving, shallow, and manipulative— much of this process is related to leading in different directions, namely, up and laterally.

Most leadership books are primarily about leading "down," influencing those who report to you or who are primarily in a following, team member role. I'd estimate that 98 percent of all the books deemed leadership fit that category. But there are far more opportunities to lead up and lead laterally for most people. This is especially true for children and youth because they have less power and status than older leaders.

When you as an adult learn how to lead up and laterally and begin benefitting from these skills, you'll typically refer to such activities using positive terms such as networking, consensus- building, relationships, and shrewd bargaining. If you don't understand the process and/or have not developed these skills, you typically refer to them in negative terms such as selling out, brown-nosing, schmoozing, and being a teacher's pet. For the most part, politics is primarily relationships, taking the time and knowing how to establish connections with people possessing various types of power and influence. Understanding how to get along with others, trading wants, and accomplishing your goals through others' influence is all about leading—but not in the conventional sense.

When we fail to understand the dynamics of leading up and laterally, we feel victimized, blaming our situation on those in power or those better at something than us. By seeing a different perspective and training our children how to lead this way, we'll provide a strategic set of tools that will benefit them throughout life.

Perhaps the biggest reason to teach young leaders about leading up and laterally is because that is what they'll be doing primarily until the ages of twenty-five to thirty-five, when most leaders begin leading down in our society. Quite often, those promoted to roles of leading down are astute at leading up and laterally. Although lesser skilled peers don't like that and yell "foul," savvy leaders realize it's a matter of knowing how to influence in different ways. The KidLead logo (on the cover of the book) denotes this with four arrows pointing in different directions, reflecting that leadership is active and multi-directional.

If your child does not have a strong leadership aptitude, learning to lead up and laterally is important, since there's a good chance s/he will be doing more of this throughout his or her life than leading down. This is a strategic way of being significant in the leadership process without being the primary leader. Many people have made lucrative livings by learning how to connect those with power and influence. Even though I realize that this book is primarily for parents and adults who work with kids with leadership aptitude, understanding how leadership works is important for everyone. It lessens the chance that your child will feel like a victim as s/he gets older, wondering why certain people get to be in charge and get their way in social settings. This education is a type of power.

Backseat Leading

We also call leading up *backseat leading*. If you're like most parents, you know what it's like to have the children in the back of the van around mealtime. "Where do you want to eat?" you ask.

"McDonald's," comes the response.

"Oh no, we've been there too much lately. Pick someplace else."

"No, we want McDonald's," echoes the reply. After a few more interactions, you find yourself in the drive-up window at the golden arches.

Were your children driving the van? No, you were. You had the power to go where you wanted, but they influenced you from the backseat.

Backseat leading for kids is about understanding who has the steering wheel at school, on the team, or in the family, and how to use that person's power to get things you want done. Sometimes it is as simple as asking. At other times it's being nice to that person and providing something they want, such as information, an offer to help, or even a compliment. There is nothing wrong with this. Knowing how to tap other people's power through relational skills is the key. Money investors refer to OPM, other people's money, a way to make a profit without risking their assets. Savvy leaders often get things done with OPI, other people's influence.

Sometimes you may not have direct access to the person with power. In that case, you need to know that person's "gatekeeper." Who keeps that person's appointment calendar? Who can forward a message to that person? Who is a friend, family member, or confidant who can put in a good word for you, make an introduction, or at least communicate an idea that you want the leader to have? Leading is about accomplishing things through other people. It is not wrong unless it's done with negative intentions. Since any of us can only know and meet so many people at a given time, we need to rely on the few who have access to people of influence.

The next time your child comes home from school and begins complaining about the teacher's unfair treatment in class, talk to him about the idea of leading up.

"Honey, why do you think the teacher didn't let your team do its project in the workroom at school?"

"Because she doesn't like us," your child says.

"Why did she let the other group do it?" you ask.

"Because she likes them more," he responds.

"What if we brainstormed some things you might be able to do to let her know that your team would like to be good and use the workroom for your project next time?"

You begin a list of ideas that might look like this:

- Ask the teacher why she let the other team use the workroom.
- Ask her what it would take for our team to use the workroom to do our project.
- Say, "If our team works really hard today, would it be okay if

we used the workroom tomorrow or with the next project?
- Offer to stay after school and help her clean the room to demonstrate support.
- See if she needs any errands run before, during, or after school, to communicate that I like her and want to help.
- Show that I am trustworthy by making sure our team's project is really good.

Sometimes, there's little difference between a person leading up and someone just schmoozing an individual with authority and power. The biggest difference tends to be in motive. If you're just interested in using another person for personal gain, then it is questionable, but if you're doing it to benefit others as a leader, then it's a matter of leading up.

> **KidLead Idea:** *When your child asks you for something, and your first response is to say no, talk about how s/he might negotiate a deal. Share something that you'd like in exchange for your child's wish. Give and take a few times. This teaches negotiating skills and thinking of others. This is proactive and productive, whereas whining and complaining are not. While this type of one-on-one interaction may not be leadership as we've defined it, this is the same skill set needed when the young leader interacts with others.*

Leading Laterally

The rook playing piece in chess can move up and down as well as sideways. The same is true with an effective leader. Moving sideways has to do with negotiating power or rights from someone who is somewhat equal to you. This might be a sibling, classmates, or neighborhood friends. In the adult world, this translates into work colleagues, peers in a social club, and neighbors.

Lateral leading is relationally based and involves understanding the interests, needs, strengths, and resources of others. The commercial equivalent is bartering. Instead of one person buying another's service or products, two parties agree to swap different items having equivalent value. For example, let's say that you're an accountant whose car needs repair. You go to your friend the mechanic and say, "I'll do your tax returns for you if you fix my car."

"Hmm," your friend says, "your car needs some parts, so what if I barter the labor, but you pay for the parts at my cost?"

"Okay, that sounds good," you say.

The goal is to think of what the other person can do or provide for you in exchange for something you might provide for him or her. This type of skill becomes leading when it is not just for personal gain but is a part of a group goal.

How do you teach this to kids? Your fourth grader comes home from school and starts whining about her and her friends not being able to play on the jungle gym because a group of fourth grade boys were using it during recess, and they always seem to get there first. You could tell her to figure out how to beat the boys there, or tattle to the teacher. But a leadership skill would be to determine who the leader is among the fourth grade boys and then talk to him about either sharing the jungle gym, being included in their game, or negotiating a trade that makes sense for both. It could even be something as simple as being friendly to the boys' leader. While you may get a few "yucks" or "ooooo's" from your child, you'll be planting the seeds of how to negotiate as a leader.

The same skills can be used at home between siblings and friends as a child learns to barter and negotiate with others in order to get what s/he wants. This skill is easily transferred into the leadership realm, where groups of people are striving to accomplish things and need to work among themselves and deal with other individuals and groups who possess power and resources that can help them accomplish their goal.

Tom Shulte, leadership trainer

I grew up in a large Catholic family, the middle of nine kids. I had three sisters and one brother who were older than me and three sisters and one brother younger than me. My dad was a chemical engineer and a natural teacher. Therefore, he made everything we did into a group task. I began to realize that I was a leader around the ages of eleven and twelve. I disliked certain chores like washing the dishes and doing the laundry. We were given the opportunity to organize ourselves, so I delegated different roles to my younger and older siblings. At the time, I just thought it was a way to get out of the work myself. I came to realize that it was leading because I was motivating them and helping them find tasks.

Social Banking

Leadership trainers talk about the concept of social banking. The idea is that all relationships have intangible accounts established that are similar to a tangible one in a real bank. When you and I come to know each other, I have an account with your name on it, and you have an account with my name. When I support you, prove trustworthy, affirm and help you, I am depositing credits into this account with my name on it. When I make requests of you, let you down, or offend you, I'm withdrawing credits from my account. I can make withdrawals until I am overdrawn. You may extend a line of credit and allow me to continue withdrawing based on my credit rating or your leniency in providing credit. The latter is often referred to as grace. But unless I begin making larger deposits than withdrawals, I'll eventually go bankrupt, and our relationship will end—account closed.

While social banking is commonly thought of in terms of leading down, it also has to do with leading up and laterally. A leader creates enough trust and goodwill among others so that she can then ask them to do things (making a withdrawal). A young leader must first invest sufficient time, energy, and good actions in the mind of a person with power in order to make a withdrawal and ask for a favor. You can illustrate this concept to your child in a number of ways, from coins in a piggy bank, to milk in a glass, to air in a balloon. The principle is that you have to put some in before you get some out. The more you put in, the more you can get out, as a general rule.

Occasionally, you meet people who don't seem to ever let you withdraw. When you run across one of these folks, you usually need to move on because their deposit or withdrawal mechanism may be broken. By talking about this with young leaders when teachable moments arise, you'll help empower them to be more effective with those who have power and authority and decrease the chance that they will feel trapped or powerless.

Laurie Beth Jones, bestselling author of *The Path* and *Jesus, CEO*, tells Kidlead about the importance of listening to young leaders who sense their ability.

It's so important to start young in helping kids discover their path and destiny. I declared at age ten that I'd be a writer and have a horse ranch. Adults often don't listen to their kids. I've met a lot of great achievers who knew what they wanted to do early. But nothing affects the life of a child so much as an unlived life of a parent. Jesus knew what he was to do at twelve. He was in line to be a carpenter, but he broke out. We see many adults in all professions who took up a mission of their parent but didn't fit them. If children are listened to and asked the right questions, much can be revealed and nurtured so they can prosper in what they're designed to do.

Discussion Activators

1. Discuss a recent example in your life when you saw leading up or leading laterally demonstrated.

2. Why do you think more attention and training are not given to these types of leading?

3. Discuss a recent situation when you could have begun to teach leading up or laterally to your child.

A hundred years from now it will not matter what your bank account was, the sort of house you lived in, or the kind of car you drove...but the world will be different because you were important in the life of a young leader.

Chapter 11

Saying "No" to Bad Leaders

Why Everyone Needs to Understand Leadership

We've all been marked by the results of good leaders and bad ones. Learning how to identify good leaders is vital, whether we are identifying a schoolyard activist, a city council nominee, or a CEO candidate. History is full of stories of leaders gone wild, convincing people to do reckless and evil deeds. Looking back, we ask, "Why didn't somebody do something? Why did people follow them?"

Although so far in this section we've been discussed an array of practical skills for developing young leaders, I wanted to include a chapter that provides a foundation for equipping both young leaders as well as those who may not have strong leadership aptitude. The principle of this chapter becomes extremely practical as you consider the importance of preparing children to deal with people in roles of power who are unethical and potentially destructive to organizations and others in general.

Classic, early psychological studies show how influential perceived authority figures can be. Today's standards would not allow these exact experiments, but they are intriguing, nonetheless. Normal people volunteering in an alleged question-answer experiment delivered deadly levels of electrical shock because a person in a white lab coat with a clipboard instructed them to do so. Is it any wonder so many people fell in line when Nazi leaders told otherwise kind, normal people to exterminate millions of Jews during World War II? Naturally, there were numerous extenuating circumstances surrounding this dark period in history, but one can imagine how intimidating Nazis officials could be. Would a broad understanding of the mechanics of leadership have helped avoid these atrocities? Perhaps not entirely, but certainly it would have in part.

At the beginning of this book, we suggested that leading is like most other aptitudes where a small percent possess a high capacity to learn it, quite a few can pick up leadership skills, and the rest are led most of their lives. And as we stated before, we believe you can do a disservice to children by trying to get them to be or do something that is not in their wiring, whether it's academics, athletics, arts, or leading.

Parents and teachers of young leaders also have young non-leaders in their lives. While we want to teach leadership skills to those with aptitude, every child should receive a basic understanding of how leadership works. Because such ignorance exists as to how leaders wield their influence, get people to work together, and move them toward united goals, far too many bad leaders have scarred the soul of civilization. Whether it's the local group of bullies at school, the corporate scandal of the week, or dictatorial warlords, rarely do these leaders make their decisions in a vacuum. Nearly always there are those who enable them to destroy the organizations they were to serve.

One example is the growing problem of gangs. I live not far from an area infested with gang crime issues and have begun working with city and school agencies to identify and develop preteen influencers before they become apprentices for gang leadership. I believe that if we identify the young natural leaders and give them ethical leadership training, we can curb gangs by shutting off the supply of organizers. Until we do that, we'll forever be pursuing reactive measures, such as better metal detectors in schools, increasing law enforcement, and expanding prison capacities. As dire as it may sound, bad leaders will always exist. The only option other than catching them early and guiding them along right paths is to inoculate the vast majority who'll otherwise end up following them. Perhaps a combination of both is the best strategy.

One way to immunize your children from the influence of bad leaders is to use the lessons and techniques provided in this book. The primary difference between teaching those with an aptitude for leading and those with little observable aptitude is your expectations. Keep them reasonable, and don't express disappointment if your teaching does not seem to result in the more significant behavior changes you'll likely see in children with more of an inclination to lead.

But just as playing flag football with a non-athletic child can help him or her better appreciate football on television, your education of how people influence each other in both good and bad ways will better prepare your child for the world of leaders brokering their wares. Followers begin empowerment by understand how leadership functions and specifically what they should do when they encounter a bad leader.

If we teach people to recognize bad leaders and say "no" to them, we will render these leaders powerless, and power is the key ingredient of any effective leading. This begins in early childhood as parents talk to their kids as opportunities arise. When the preschool bully picks on your child, talk to her at her level and explain that certain people do bad things that hurt people. This is not right. When a person continues to do bad things, that person should be confronted. Talk to your teacher, your principal, or another adult and ask them to stop the bully. An alternative is to talk to a few classmates and organize them to talk to the teacher, coach, or principal.

Identifying the Bully-Leader

Bullying is becoming a problem that is being addressed in schools. You can find several books and websites on the topic if you google it. One survey of nine- to thirteen-year-olds revealed that 86 percent of kids said they've seen someone bullied, 48 percent reported being bullied, and 42 percent admitted bullying at least once in a while.* Kids suffer from the behavior of both individual bullies and gangs of hoodlums who tease and intimidate. This is little different from what happens in the grown-up world when ruthless managers, intimidating bosses, and unscrupulous CEOs run their organizations by fear. The big difference is that these experiences can dent the self-image and confidence of a person who is still moldable.

Whistle-blowing is now a legally protected action in government and many companies. When leaders go wild, people need the freedom to hold them accountable without fear of retaliation. Perhaps as bad as being bullied is being persuaded to follow a bully-leader. As the wise saying goes, "Evil company corrupts good habits." Here are some indicators of bad leaders that you can begin to teach your children so they can avoid befriending them, which is often the precursor to a child becoming a follower of that bully-leader. The five qualities form the acrostic "AVOID."

- Asks you to do things that you know are wrong.
- Very open about not liking authority figures, such as teachers and police.
- Openly teases others and makes them feel afraid.
- Involved with other people who are not nice.
- Does things that you know are not right.

Sometimes, children come home and tell stories about kids who are bullied at school. One thing you can do to empower your child is to provide ideas for responding to this situation. Stronger leaders can confront a bully who may be trying to "mark" his territory by intimidating a new student to prove himself among his followers. Another option is to respond by inviting the bullied child to participate in a game or activity that takes attention away from the student and provides the strength of numbers and association with a good leader. Bullies typically seek children who are alone or whom they perceive to be weak and vulnerable.

Identifying Good Influencers

Merely pointing out bad leaders in order to avoid them and help hold them accountable isn't enough. The proactive approach involves helping your child discover peers who are good leaders. The more you can foster friendships among young leaders who seem stable, healthy, and positive, the more apt you are to create an awareness of good leadership in your child. This can result in a child's conscious choice to hook her wagon to stars so she rises along with the leader. Good leaders know who their best followers are and strive to find places for them as they develop. There are many stories of renowned leaders who met their closest colleagues in college and as young adults. When you find a leader worth following, you'll benefit from aligning with him or her. Here are some indicators of a young, good leader.

- The young person exhibits many of the leader indicators explained in Chapter 2.
- S/he is respectful of adults and those in authority.
- S/he stands up against people and principles that are destructive.
- S/he comes from a home that exudes strong values.
- The young person demonstrates responsibility.

Go out of your way to help your child build a relationship with this type of individual. While you can't force a friendship, you can foster them and improve the chances of the young leader knowing and liking your child. This will also increase the likelihood that s/he will learn to identify a good leader and avoid a bad one. Parents lax in controlling who their child hangs out with are setting up their child to lose. Be bold. Show parental leadership by not being intimidated by complaining and resistance when you push or prevent certain relationships. The bottom line is that families can do a lot to determine the success of their child, specifically by influencing who is influencing them.

The more people who understand the dynamics of leadership and how leaders get people to work together to accomplish goals, the less effective bad leaders will be. Because there is power in numbers, the more who stand up to bad leaders and refuse to participate in their vision, the less effective the leaders will be. The greatest power a leader has is in the people who follow. Remove your allegiance from the mix, and you reduce a leader's power. When this happens over and over, a bad leader can be rendered powerless.

> ***KidLead Idea:*** *Bullying is one of the most common child/ preteen movie themes. Watch a movie with your child that depicts a bully-leader. There are many, such as* <u>Holes</u>, <u>The Incredibles</u>, <u>Monsters Inc.</u>, <u>Ants</u>, <u>The Ant Bully</u>, <u>Pinocchio</u> *and others. As you watch the movie, push pause after a scene where the bully taunts others or tries to get his or her gang of followers to pick on someone. Talk about the scene using what you've learned in this chapter.*

> Ken Blanchard, bestselling co-author of the *One Minute Manager* series, tells KidLead about the importance of starting leadership training young.
>
> I think it is vital to train kids how to be responsible leaders. I meet far too many adult leaders who obviously didn't have good childhood development, who didn't turn out well. I think that a lot of the books that I've written are very teachable to young people because they're important concepts taught in a story or parable style.
>
> We tried to teach our kids to be good leaders. They didn't always seem to appreciate it at the time, but they learned it. I'm convinced that kids cannot only understand how to lead effectively, but they can do it faster and better than their parents. But you have to be smart about the way you do it. You can't just tell them what to do and teach them to be dependent on you.

Discussion Activators

1. Tell a story of a bad leader in your past who was a negative influence in your life and/or the lives of others.

2. Brainstorm other things you can do as a parent to teach your child how to identify and avoid bad leaders.

3. List a few good young leaders you know with whom you can help your child foster a potential friendship.

*2004 Kids Health KidsPoll survey of 1,200 9-13 year old boys and girls. www.kidshealth.org

Section III.

⌘ ⌘ ⌘

Developing Young Leaders: Content

Leadership is not so much in words, as in

attitude and in actions.

-Harold Geneen, Chairman, ITT Corp.

Chapter 12

Four Key Leader Relationship Skills

Begin with the End in Mind

Michelangelo said that when he saw a block of marble, he envisioned the statue trying to get out. His job as a sculptor was simply to remove the unnecessary stone. The genius began his work, imagining the finished product. If we want to raise effective and ethical leaders, we need to begin with the end in mind. What types of leaders do we want influencing our corporations, faith communities, and government? If you look at the research by the Center for Creative Leadership, Harvard, and other respected researchers, you'll come up with a lot of qualities that people look for in those they want to follow. One list has as many as 120. But when you're beginning fresh, where do you begin?

Any number of personal qualities is important to becoming a well-rounded, self-actualized individual, but there are some that are essential to leading. Based on my doctoral work and a review of a lot of other research, plus working with hundreds of leaders for over fifteen years, we've come up with an essentials list of core qualities that we teach young leaders in **Lead**Now and **Lead**Well, training programs of KidLead. We believe that if young leaders begin to capture these qualities, they'll be equipped with the tools to become responsible leaders whom others want to follow. If leaders are missing these basics, they will either implode or be rendered impotent. When leaders fail, it's typically due to inadequacies in one or more of these sixteen qualities, featured in the pie chart below.

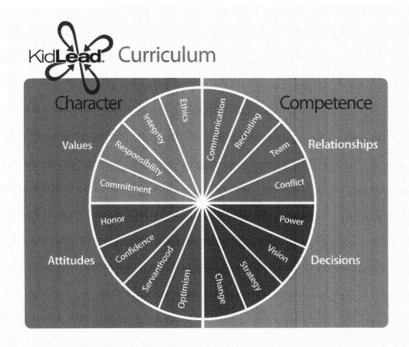

Among these qualities, approximately half reflect character-oriented themes, (left half of graph) and the other half lean toward competencies or skills (right side). Of the character qualities, four are value-related and four attitudinal. Of the competencies, four are relational themes and four are decision-oriented. These are convenient, not rigid divisions, but they provide a structure to help organize an intentional training program.

The purpose of Chapters 12-15 is to give adults working with children and youth a framework for knowing what to emphasize, instead of wandering in a fog. Having an end in mind as you work with your young leaders will help you gain direction on how to get there. You can develop an alternative list, but be sure to include these sixteen qualities if you want to grow great leaders.

We will briefly define each of these sixteen qualities at the preteen level, establish their importance, and then provide some ideas of how you can teach these qualities in the context of leadership, not just as individual characteristics. The ideas are to "prime the pump" as you develop your own home lessons. In this chapter, we'll focus on the four key leader relational skills, and Chapter 13 covers the four key leader decision skills. Chapter 14 introduces four key leader character values, and Chapter 15 covers the four key leader character attitudes.

Relationships

Effective leaders balance task-orientation with people-orientation. Go too far either way and results diminish. But leaders fail the most in the relational arena. Leading is a social art, so being able create a team, knowing how to get people in the right places, and communicating and then resolving conflicts that arise are all vital skills. The following are summaries and *pump primers*, ideas for adult to use in teaching these relational skills that are depicted in the upper right quarter of the previous graph.

Quality: Team Building

Concept: Many hands accomplish much. *A good leader builds a team.*
The primary purpose of this quality is to recognize the power of a team over that of working as an individual. Although we placed it in the relational skill quarter, it is fundamental to leading in general. Individuals can accomplish wonderful things, but teamwork allows us to achieve what we could not alone. Like the acrostic says, TEAM: Together Everyone Accomplishes More. The leader's job is to develop teams and help them function effectively. As you teach this concept, point out situations in everyday life that illustrate the power of people working together to accomplish things.

Pump Primers:
- The next time you watch or participate in a team sport, talk about how the players function together and what it might be like if the other team only had one person.
- Listen to a symphony. Describe the sounds of the different instruments, and discuss how the conductor helps them play together.

- The next time you drive in your car, discuss how it was built, planned by designers and engineers, built by mechanics, and sold by salespeople.
- When you sit at a restaurant, ask your child to identify the different roles of the staff, along with what the experience would be like if someone were missing or not doing his or her job effectively.
- When you go to a team-oriented movie, talk about the characters in the film. You can also discuss the film and what it took to get it to us as consumers.

Summary: When you discuss a school or work situation, bring in the concept of a team, and talk about how people combine their time, skills, interests, and talents to create what none of us could alone. In each situation, remember to mention the role of leaders, who set direction for teams and help people use their abilities, get along together, and stay on course. Everyday life is filled with situations where people do individual tasks in cooperation with others, resulting in much larger accomplishments.

> **KidLead Idea:** *Here's a fun way to teach the importance of the team. You need 3 or more people along with a box of paper clips. Give each child 30 seconds to link as many paper clips as possible into their own chain as individuals. They can only use single clips. Ask everyone to count his or her total and determine the average length. Then instruct everyone to work together to make the longest chain possible in 30 seconds with individual clips. You may provide a little time for them to get organized. Then count the total and contrast it with the average of the individual scores. Discuss the difference.*

Quality: Recruits Talent

Concept: People want to win. *A good leader helps people use their strengths.*

Inviting people to be a part of a team is important because we've all been on teams where people were in the wrong roles or we felt underutilized. Plus, we've likely experienced the problem of having too few people to accomplish a job and the challenge of getting people to join our team. That is the primary theme of recruiting.

Pump Primers:
- When you go into a store that has a "Now Hiring" sign, talk about what that means and how organizations find people to work for them. Discuss the importance of leaders asking the right people to fill positions on the team.
- During a live or televised team sports event, discuss what it would be like if the coach changed the player's positions. What if the catcher became the pitcher? "If you were the coach of your team, who would you put in the different places?"
- When you're discussing a work situation around your kids, talk to them about recruiting. "Mommy's frustrated at her job right now because we have someone who isn't doing his job very well. That makes it difficult for everyone else. Here's who we need…"
- When a machine (car, TV, computer) breaks down, talk about what happens when team members fail in a project or task.
- Part of leading is the "task of ask," looking people in the eye and seeking commitment. Practice the basic skills of this by having your child make a request at a restaurant or store when you'd normally do it as the parent. "Excuse me, sir, but could I have a clean glass. This seems to be dirty."

Summary: Recruiting often involves selling a person on participating with the team, striving to reach its goal, and believing in his or her strengths. This requires the combination of assessing what kind of talent is needed, analyzing a person's ability, and then motivating him or her to participate. This is the equivalent of what Jim Collins calls "getting the right people in the right seats on the bus." This is vital for effective organizations.

> **KidLead Idea:** *An important part of recruiting is identifying a person's strengths. This begins with identifying the leader's strengths. Help your child discover hi or her strengths.*
> *You can find a simple 1-page list that we use in one of our* **Lead***Now lessons if you go to www.kidlead.com, click on*

"Resources," and then "Strengths List." Have your child select the four top strengths and then write these on a blank wooden block you can get at craft stores, one per side. This becomes a reminder you can place on a desk or dresser.

Nina Lewis, KidLead Certified Trainer

As I look back, I began realizing that I was a leader around eight or nine years of age. We lived on a good-sized ranch with horses, pigs, goats, and rabbits that needed feeding. I began orchestrating how the animals were fed and recruiting my younger sister and brother to do most of the manual labor. By ten to twelve years old, I was pretty good at this, which upset my parents. My brother and sister didn't mind because I rewarded them with chocolate chips, except that my mom never had them when she wanted to make cookies. By fifteen or so, I began to realize that being bossy wasn't working because no one wanted to help me anymore. My sister used to get up early and make sandwiches for school, but I got so picky, she quit making them for me. I realized I needed to respect and honor people if I wanted them to help.

Quality: Effective Communicator

Concept: Teams thrive on communication. *A good leader talks and listens to people.*

We've all been a part of teams and organizations where communication was poor and as a result, people were offended, customers left, and plans failed. Leaders need to realize that just because ideas are in their heads, everyone else doesn't know what they're thinking. At the same time, many assume the job of leading is telling people what to do. But good leaders are also adept listeners who allow team members to feel heard. Multiple ideas improve outcomes. When communication breaks down, teams suffer.

Pump Primers:
- The next time you have a family miscommunication, ask your child how to improve communication in the future. Then discuss why leaders need to communicate well.
- Assign one- to three-minute speeches where you reward your child for doing a formal talk to family members, adding other

listeners as confidence increases. This may be telling a story about losing a tooth, participating in a fun school event, or starting a "best story of the week" tradition after dinner. The more presentations a leader does, the easier it becomes and the better s/he gets.

- Practice listening skills by using an item like a big spoon or goofy alternative and creating a rule that only the person holding it can speak. The rest have to listen until they signal to get it.
- Most kids consider their parents as leaders. Model the importance of a leader listening by allotting a set period of time when only the children can talk and the parent can only ask questions.
- Create a written template for events in your family, whether it's a ball game, dentist appointment, business trip, or concert. Include essentials such as: Who, What, When, Where, and How. Post these sheets of paper for home projects, vacations, and weekly events that involve multiple people. This teaches the responsibility of including essential information for those involved.

Summary: Family life provides a lot of opportunities to practice communication skills and explain why they are important in leadership. Formal speaking, listening, and including sufficient information are vital. The challenge tends to be figuring out a constructive time to talk about it, since teachable moments tend to be when people are irritated, making learning more difficult. Therefore, try to discuss communication issues when everyone is in a good mood so that when there's a breakdown, you can remind everyone how difficult as well as how important it is to have teamwork and leadership.

> **KidLead Idea:** *Here's a fun way to experience the challenge of limited information: leadership Pictionary. A person draws a sketch of an item that others try to guess. You can't use words or motions. Pictures might include: team, President, goal, talking, listening, etc. Then discuss how challenging communication can be for leaders when there are limitations.*

Quality: Handles Conflict

Concept: Teams create differing ideas. *A good leader helps teams stay united.*

Whenever people work together, they will have different ideas on how to accomplish the task, not to mention unique personalities and idiosyncrasies. Leading includes pushing against the status quo and requiring change. As a result, there is conflict. The key is in how a leader deals with it. A divided team doesn't work well together. Leading weaknesses include: creating unnecessary conflict due to a lack of people skills, squelching healthy conflict that is a natural part of processing, and letting conflict become dysfunctional by not effectively addressing it.

Pump Primers:
- After the next family conflict, be very intentional about unpacking the various feelings, opinions, and actions of those involved. Take the role of a neutral arbitrator or reporter. This allows a young leader to discuss his or her feelings in an emotionally safe setting so that when pressures rise again, s/he can respond more effectively.
- Conflict is a common theme in movies and TV shows. The next time you see a scene where there is conflict, discuss the people involved, the reasons for the conflict, and possible options for reducing it.
- Emotional intelligence is important for leaders to be effective. This involves identifying personal emotions as well as those of others. Ask your child to write down how each person might be feeling during a conflict, as writing exacts a person's thinking.
- People often express emotions of anger when they feel helpless, like victims. When your child comes to you with a frustration over a friend or sibling, brainstorm responses and estimate outcomes so that the young leader can choose the most productive way to respond to his or her emotions.

Summary: The primary goal in handling conflict well is effective resolution, not avoidance. By modeling empathetic listening and not overreacting to emotions of anger, we equip leaders to resolve differing perspectives on teams.

KidLead Idea: During conflict, leaders can use words that hurt people, even after the discussion is over. Cut out a paper gingerbread person. Take turns saying words people use that hurts us. Each time a hurtful word is used, tear off a piece of the paper person. After doing this 6-8 times, use masking tape (not invisible tape) and repair the person. Then discuss how tearing the paper person is like a leader using words that hurt others.

Discussion Activators

1. Can you think of examples to demonstrate when leaders failed in the areas of these four competencies? What are they?

2. Why is it important to look for real-life situations where young leaders can gain better understanding of these key skills?

Chapter 13

Four Key Leader Decision Skills

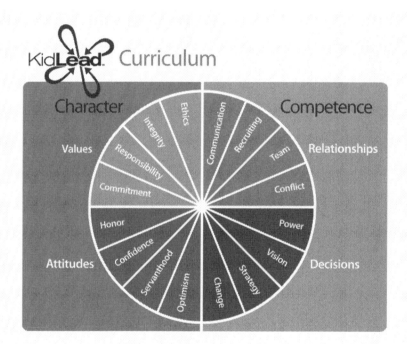

Decisions

Leaders are decision makers. The quality of their decisions not only impacts themselves, but it affects those around them. That is why leaders need to become effective decision makers, embracing responsibility of the bigger picture. Seeking and using power effectively, knowing how to communicate an inspiring vision, developing a strategy, and pursuing change are all vital decision making skills that leaders need to possess. The following are summaries and pump primers, ideas for adults to use in teaching these relational skills that are depicted in the lower right quarter of the previous graph.

Quality: Finds and Uses Power Constructively

Concept: Influence moves a team. *A good leader uses power to help others.*

Power is an inevitable part of leading. You cannot lead without it. Power comes from a variety of sources, so young leaders should begin to understand what it is, where to find it, and how to handle it. The temptation of power is to use it selfishly and to hurt people, so the goal is to help leaders know how to use it to benefit others. The more comfortable leaders are using power, the less likely they'll misuse it as they develop.

Pump Primers:
- There are several sources of power:
  - o   Resource: money, muscle, time, tools
  - o   Talent: ability, skill, experience, training
  - o   Information: knowledge, ideas, education
  - o   People: friends, network
  - o   Position: role, authority, title in company
  - o   (Parents who are faith-oriented may also want to include God and spiritual power as a category.)
  - o   Label large plastic cups with these titles, and over the course of a week, have family members drop in examples of each. Discuss them after a few days to see how the different types of power affect us, especially when working with others.
- Inevitably, you'll hear a child complaining about a teacher, principal, boss or parent. Use this as an opportunity to explain the idea of "leading up." Brainstorm ways that the person with less power can get what s/he wants by aligning with the more powerful person's interests.
- When a young leader complains about a peer or sibling, use this opportunity to explain the idea of "leading laterally."

Brainstorm ways the person complaining can get what s/he wants by aligning with the other person's interests and goals.
- There are plenty of stories of misused power in the news. Select one, and read it with your child. Discuss how the leader misused power and hurt people. Address other negative consequences and options the leader could have chosen.

Summary: The goal in teaching this quality is to understand the positive role of power in getting things done, while also realizing its potential to cause damage and hurt people through misuse. By talking about it openly and intelligently, we can reduce the frustration leaders face as adults who do not understand its importance and danger.

> **KidLead Idea:** Here's a fun activity to do with 4 or more people. Get a thick, sturdy rope and play a game of tug of war, where people on one side try to pull those hanging onto the other end of the rope across a line. Make the sides lopsided so that one is stronger each time. Then talk about power and how leaders use it to get things done. For example, a person who is the president of a company has more power than a vice-president. A vice-president would likely lose trying to change a policy that the president wanted. The strategy might be for the vice-president to convince the president that his or her idea would save the company a lot of money.

Quality: Communicates Vision

Concept: Teams thrive on inspiration. *A good leader imagines the victory before it happens.*

A vision is a preferred future; it provides a snapshot of what the goal will look like when it is accomplished. This provides a mental picture that inspires people to embrace the risk and follow the leader. Vision is one of the most difficult skills to teach, yet it is a fundamental factor that often determines whether a leader is followed or not. Being able to articulate a preferred future creates hope and excitement in potential team members. Also, vision is important for recruiting and instilling courage during difficult times.

Pump Primers:

- Listen to Martin Luther King's "I Have a Dream" speech with your young leader. Discuss why this was such an effective vision. You can find this and other great speeches online at www.americanrhetoric.com.
- A good vision statement is clear, measurable, urgent, and important. Read these three pre-game statements by coaches and discuss which ones are motivating and why:
  - o Okay, team, it's going to be tough, but let's have some fun out there today."
  - o "I think we can win this game. If everyone plays their position and does a good job, we can be proud of that."
  - o "If we work hard as a team, we can win. Not only can we win, but we can walk off the field with our heads held high. This is *your* moment! Give it your all!"
- Rent the movie, *Braveheart* and watch the freedom speech, where William Wallace (played by Mel Gibson) inspires his soldiers to defend their land and fight the opposing army. You can also find this clip on the Internet by googling it.
- Blindfold your young leader(s) and set up a maze of cones, cups, or chairs. Give verbal directions from one end to the other. Take off the blindfold so s/he can see the maze. Talk about why a clear picture is important for leaders to provide so that people can be inspired and feel confident.

Summary: Vision is the single most difficult leadership skill to teach. Much of it is intuitive. We recognize it when we hear it. Vision is more right-brained and emotional than calculated. When you experience a heartwarming event with a team or leader, take advantage of discussing vision with your child.

> **KidLead Idea:** *Assist your young leader in developing a vision statement for his or her life that includes leading. Work on a 50-word paragraph or a bulleted list that declares values, goals, and accomplishments. Print these in large font on a single sheet of paper and frame it. Update this personal vision statement each year, perhaps around a birthday. While this is a good activity for any child, it provides practice specifically for leading.*

Sean Covey, author of *Seven Habits of Successful Teens*, tells KidLead how his dad, Stephen Covey, influenced his leadership ability.

I felt like Dad always had time for me. I remember him calling the Utah Valley Athletic Association about a year in advance to find out when all the high school football games would be so he could plan his schedule around my senior year. The games weren't even scheduled yet. I remember thinking, "Wow, he cares a lot." That was a great feeling.

I remember calling him a lot when he was starting his new business, The Covey Leadership Center. Anytime I called him, he'd drop whatever he was doing, whether it was a board meeting or talking to other people. He'd always spend whatever time I needed. I felt like I could interrupt at anytime. You'd even talk with his staff, and they'd say, "Oh yeah, Stephen's told us, 'family comes first' and he'll interrupt anytime for any issue to talk to family." It gave me a feeling of power that I could interrupt whenever and that I was important.

Another thing is that he made us feel like we could do anything. He's constantly saying things such as, "You'd be a great student body president." We'd say, "I'm not good at that kind of stuff. It'd scare me to death." He'd say, "Oh you'd be great. I can't think of anyone better than you."

Dad would say, "You're really good at this kind of thing. I see you as being someone who's going to make a huge difference in the world." It's not fake. It's genuine. He sees where your talents and strengths are and paints a picture for what's possible and makes you want to go for it.

Quality: Thinks Strategically

Concept: People desire direction. *A good leader develops a plan with a team.*

A strategy is a plan that connects the current situation with the preferred future of the vision. It is what tethers a dream to reality so that a tactical mission can be divided into specific roles, resources, and responsibilities. Many leaders lack strategy. Others try to develop strategy in a vacuum, failing to gain buy-in from would be followers. Young leaders need to develop the "how" of accomplishing a goal or task, not just the "what" it is we're trying to accomplish.

Pump Primers:
- Create a "to do" list with your young leader that includes events for his or her week. Then, to teach time prioritization skills, brainstorm strategies for accomplishing these tasks in time segments.
- The next time a family plan goes wrong, put your child in charge of leading the family in coming up with a solution or at least brainstorming options. The change could be a car breaking down, a meeting running long, or rain that cancels an event.
- Ask your young leader and three or four of their friends to design and build a structure that all of them can sit under. This structure must consist of items that everyone brings, not a tent or commercial awning. This requires them to strategize a plan, implement their plan, and make changes as needed.
- Talk to a principal, pastor, priest, or community agency for a project idea that your child can lead a team of others to accomplish. Be available as a coach, but don't run the project. Let your young leader plan it and then provide a debriefing after the project is completed.

Summary: The goal of learning strategic planning skills is twofold. A leader must first help create an initial plan. Secondly, there needs to be suitable flexibility so that changes can be made when s/he implements the plan and discovers what is and is not working. Initiating a positive revision is vital for keeping hope strong among team members.

> **KidLead Idea:** *Ask your young leader to plan a ½ day trip that would include going to at least 2 places and that requires a budget. You can set time and money limitations beforehand or after the initial plan is presented to you. Let your child lead the family throughout the trip, pausing along the way to re-strategize. Include details such as transportation, directions, assigning roles, etc. If you want*

to add a level of difficulty, include others in the strategizing phase to teach your child how to negotiate others' opinions and agendas.

Quality: Initiates Change

<u>Concept</u>: People often fear the new. *A good leader pursues constructive change.*

Leaders are catalysts, individuals who pursue opportunities that require a move away from the status quo. In order to do this, leaders must understand the natural aversion most people have toward change in general. Leaders with skills for initiating change effectively are highly valued. A common weakness of leaders is trying to sell a solution before there's a perceived problem. They fail to understand the emotional price of change in people, such as fear, grieving what is lost, and anger. Leaders take a proactive approach to both initiating and responding to change.

<u>Pump Primers</u>**:**
- Stand back to back to another person. Instruct each person to change something about his or her appearance in fifteen to twenty seconds. Then turn around and try to guess what each other changed. Do this two to three times. Discuss the concept of change and a leader's role in seeing the need for it.
- Talk about a pending family change or a relocation the child remembers. List the challenges and benefits. Discuss how a good leader is honest about these as s/he discusses them with people but emphasizes the benefits.
- The next time a young leader is complaining about school, a sports team, or family situation, take time to brainstorm a solution. Better yet, give the child an assignment. If you were the principal/teacher/parent, what would you do and why?
- Plan a family outing or date with your young leader. State the plan. Then, intentionally make changes, such as the timing, destination, amount of money available, etc. Teach the concept of flexibility and resilience. End on a fun note with a favorite dessert as you discuss a leader's response to changes in plans.

Summary: Change is what leaders pursue with others for the benefit of an organization or group. The goal is to help young leaders understand the emotional challenge people experience when leaders pursue change, along with potential costs and benefits. Seize family changes to discuss this in order to reduce the fear of leading change.

> **KidLead Idea:** *Here's a fun activity, but you'll need to weigh the pros and cons of it given your young leader's personality and family agreements on messing with people's "stuff." When your young leader is away, go into his or her room and rearrange it, from pictures on the walls to furnishings or even switching rooms. Then announce a surprise and introduce the change. Discuss the feelings, as most changes create common emotional responses in people.*

While you could break down these eight qualities into sub-skills, helping young leaders understand what these are and how they function will create a mindset that allows a leader to develop other skills as s/he matures.

Discussion Activators

1. Name examples of leaders failing in these four competencies.

2. Provide one specific example of something that happened to you this week that illustrates one of these four qualities.

Chapter 14

Four Key Leader Character Values

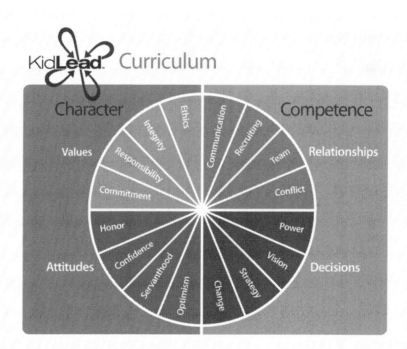

The Tangible Intangibles

Character is often summarized as who we are, competence as what we can do well. Character is important to leaders because it affects what they do; in turn, their actions impact many beyond themselves. CEOs who siphon money for themselves, religious leaders who betray, and presidents who break the rules to win favors cause people to lose their jobs and retirement, require counseling, file lawsuits, and avoid trusting future leaders. Character is directly related to values and decision making, which in turn impacts organizations measurably. The intangibles of character nearly always result in tangible impact. When leaders are involved, the results are multiplied.

Your goal is a parent or young leader-developer is to intersect character with leading so that young leaders understand how the values we hold as leaders directly impact how we function and the people and organizations we serve. Discussing this as adults is one thing, but communicating intangibles to preteens and younger is quite another. This and the next chapter deal with the eight leader qualities that are character-oriented.

Values

A value is a core belief that provides guidance for decision making and determines how a leader conducts himself or herself. It is equivalent to an operating system in a computer. While people possess any number of values and most parents have a conscious or unconscious list of these, four emerge as the ones where leaders fail most often and, therefore, become strategic for effective leading. The following are summaries of leader ethics, integrity, responsibility, and commitment, along with pump primers, ideas for adult to use in teaching these relational skills that are depicted in the upper left quarter of the previous graph.

Quality: Ethical

Concept: A leader's decisions affect others. *A good leader does what is right.*

This is more of a practical than philosophical definition. Ethics has to do with how a leader operates personally and makes decisions that affect the team. When a leader lowers her standards, compromises on legal issues, and practices situational ethics, team members are at first confused but then follow suit. The result is turmoil throughout the organization. This is a growing issue in a global market, where one culture's ethical standards differ from another's.

<u>Pump Primers</u>**:**
- Movies and storybooks commonly include evil rulers. The next time you're watching a film or reading a book, pause to discuss what specifically the leader did that was unethical and why this was wrong. Was there deception, stealing, cheating, or killing?
- Offer to reward your young leader for reporting on one or more newspaper stories where a leader who lacked high standards made a decision that affected others. The key is to focus on leaders versus individuals. Have your child tell you about the leader, the decision, and the consequences.
- Clarify and state your own house rules. Perhaps come up with a draft list that you discuss as a family. Then print them and place them in a frame for all family members to see. You can refer to this when discrepancies arise. For example, "The Nelsons honor each other. We will be truthful with each other."

*Summary***:** There are basic ethical issues that transcend cultures and religions. Obviously, if you're faith-oriented, you'll want to weave in spiritual values that influence leadership ethics. If not, there are universal standards in society that are consistently recognized, such as honesty, fairness, and honor.

> ***KidLead Idea:*** *Gather 2-3 young leaders to build cardboard sheds. You're going to provide different length rulers to use, without them knowing it. Before the activity, make 1 homemade, paper or cardboard ruler per team. Construct one with twelve 1-inch units, one with 1.5-inch units, and one with 2-inch units. You may want to separate the kids. Provide 1-2 sheets of poster board, tape, scissors, and the following instructions:*
>
> *You only have 15 minutes to build a shed according to the following blueprint instructions, so you'll need to work quickly. Only use the cardboard ruler that was given to your team for measuring.*

Step 1: Measure, draw, and cut 2 sidewalls: 6 units tall by 9 units long.

Step 2: Measure, draw, and cut 2 front and back walls: 6 units tall by 6 units wide.

Step 3: Attach these together with tape.

Step 4: Measure, draw, and cut a roof: 10 units wide by 10 units long; bend it slightly in the middle and attach it to the top of the walls. (There will be an open space between the roof and the front and back walls. This is a shed, not a house.)

Step 5: Feel free to decorate your shed until the time is up.

After everyone is finished, compare the differences in size, and then discuss the reason for this and how it relates leaders and the standards they use in leading. The reason that the sheds were different sizes is that each leader used a different standard for measuring the pieces. Similarly, when one leader says it is okay to cheat and another does not, they will come up with different decisions that, in turn, affect the outcomes and everyone on the team.

Josh Nelson, on upholding standards socially

During my freshman year in college, I organized a dress-up Christmas party because we didn't have many opportunities like that. I recruited a group of people to bring food and music, and make sure that others got invited. A lot of people came. When a few students arrived without being dressed up, I talked to them, telling them that they needed to leave unless they put on collared shirts. I felt like they needed to comply with the standards we'd established and with what the others were doing. A few of them changed their clothes and returned, and a few left and didn't come back. One guy came drunk and started swearing, so a couple of us confronted him and asked him to leave. The people who attended had a great time and seemed to appreciate that we provided a nice environment for them.

Quality: Acts with Integrity

Concept: Teams need to trust leaders. *Good leaders do what they say.*

Ethics and integrity are related. The word "integrity" literally refers to wholeness, completeness, not being divided in your values or standards. A lot of it has to do with dependability based on a person's actions being aligned with his or her beliefs. Integrity is more about the leader's personal life that impacts how s/he influences others. For example, a leader lacking integrity will make promises to team members that are not kept, resulting in people getting mad or quitting the team. Consistently matching "walk with talk" develops a deep trust between leaders and their team members.

Pump Primers:
- Consider intentionally breaking one of your own family standards in order to provide a teachable moment as a leader. Perhaps it is skipping a commitment you made to go out for ice cream, forgetting or refusing to pay an allowance, or making your children clean their room while yours is a mess. After the experience, discuss the importance of keeping one's word as a leader. Then try to make it right.
- Gather at least two people and your young leader for a cup stacking competition. Challenge each person or team to build the tallest tower of plastic cups they can in five minutes. Unevenly divide the cups without letting them know this. One might have twenty, another thirty, and still another forty. At the end, give an award to the winner, and then point out the difference in numbers. Discuss how things like this reduce trust in a leader.
- There will be times when your child deceives you, either by lying outright, changing the facts, or withholding information. Make a point to increase the negative consequences for deception. When you do, point out the importance of integrity, especially as a leader, as this is what trust is built on in relationships.

Summary: Although most would agree that integrity is an important character quality for all people, be aware of opportunities to point out why integrity is even more important for leaders. When people feel as though they cannot trust a leader, they are far less apt to follow him or her.

> **KidLead Idea:** *A fun way to teach this is playing "Two Truths and a Lie." Participants write three statements, 2 that are true and 1 that is not true. The others try to guess the lie by writing it down, and then the lie is revealed. The problem with the game as it's played is that it rewards deception. Therefore, at the end, emphasize the importance of being able to sense when someone is telling the truth or not, since leaders need to develop this skill when working with others.*

Quality: Responsible

Concept: Our team depends on us. *A good leader follows through*.

Leaders are responsible individuals, who carry more of the burden for a team or organization than others. That means leaders need to follow through on their word and assigned tasks more than others if they want others to do the same. When leaders behave irresponsibly, they lose the respect of others and their ability to lead. Those who drop the ball don't care and should not be followed.

Pump Primers:
- Assign a project to a young leader that includes making assignments to team members. When people follow through, teach the leader how to affirm them. If people fail, discuss how that makes a leader feel.
- Talk about the idea of accelerated responsibility. This means allowing greater reward and freedom for demonstrated follow-through. When a child has been diligent enough to be in bed at the stated time, gradually increase the time limit, explaining why.
- When a friend disappoints your child, discuss these feelings and attach them to the actions of irresponsibility. Followers feel this when their leader is irresponsible.
- When you fail to follow through as a parent, don't make excuses. Model how leaders behave when they fail to follow through. Confess, seek forgiveness, and pledge to improve.

<u>Summary</u>**:** Again, as with all of these character qualities, try to intentionally connect responsibility with leading. Use the words together as often as you can. Because a leader's strengths and weaknesses are multiplied in a team or organization, the value of responsibility is vital. Leaders who don't follow through on what they say soon lose respect from would-be followers. This diminishes their ability to lead further.

> ***KidLead Idea:*** *Parents and teachers sometimes overlook kids who are following through, calling attention to the times they fail or to those who are irresponsible. Surprise your children by spontaneously rewarding (or double-rewarding them) for following through on things they may be doing on a regular basis, whether it's making their bed, cleaning their bathroom, or doing homework. This type of reinforcement has a lasting effect and calls attention to the importance of responsibility. Catch them doing something good, and make a big deal about it.*

Quality: Committed

<u>Concept</u>: People rarely commit more than their leader. *A good leader is dedicated.*

A value related to responsibility is commitment. By this we mean genuinely caring about a task, project, or organization that a leader sells to others. Rarely is anything great ever accomplished without perseverance, preceded by and resulting from strong commitment. When a leader casts a vision but easily gives up, people give up following that leader. Some leaders are good at selling ideas but lousy on sticking with them during difficult times and making personal sacrifices they ask of others.

<u>Pump Primers</u>:
- Most kids start a sport, hobby, or big project and then want to give up when they lose interest or it becomes difficult. As much as possible, make sure your child finishes the season so that s/he values commitment and understands persevering through

the painful times. This underlies teaching commitment in the context of leading.

- When you quit a job, relationship, or project, talk as openly as possible with your child about why you are doing this as well as what you may be giving up as a result. It is very difficult to teach our kids to be committed when they see us quitting.
- Talk to your child about a project you could do together that would be significant but still attainable. Make this a "commitment project" that primarily teaches the quality of sticking with it. When you hit a tough spot, talk it through and push forward.
- If possible, read a short biography of a leader or pay your child to read it. Most leader biographies point out the value of commitment to an idea in spite of difficulty. Discuss this aspect with your child.

Here is something to consider about establishing rewards. Payment doesn't need to be monetary, but find a reward that your child enjoys. While some parents and teachers push back on external rewards, the goal is not to replace intrinsic motivation but complement it. Life tends to work that way. Think of how you'd feel accomplishing a big project for your supervisor or company without getting any type of reward or acknowledgment for your extra and/or exemplary effort. Perhaps an "A" grade is not necessary for learning, but it sure helps.

Summary: Commitment in leadership is important. But there come times when a leader needs to quit, when it would be foolish to persevere, hurt people, waste resources, and drag down the organization. This is a very sophisticated concept, even for adults. More leadership projects fail by not persevering than any single factor. A leader's commitment to the team and task are vital to the outcome.

> **KidLead Idea:** *Think of a movie that illustrates the value of commitment, and have a movie night, making sure to spend at least 5 minutes talking about the value. If the film illustrates individual commitment as opposed to leadership, then tie in the importance of this value to leading.*
> *Examples:* The Incredibles, Wall-E *(individual commitment),*

<u>Holes, Tucker, Remember the Titans, Miracle,</u> *and* <u>Hoosiers</u>.

Discussion Activators

1. What examples can you think of when leaders failed in the areas of these four competencies?

2. As you read the ideas on teaching these qualities, did any others come to mind?

Chapter 15

Four Key Leader Character Attitudes

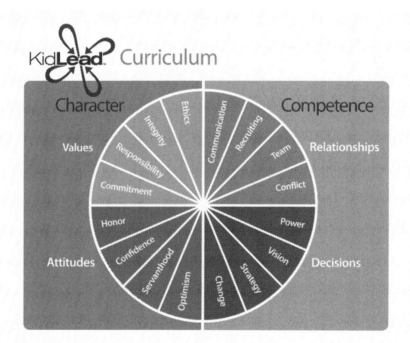

Attitudes

An attitude is a way of thinking that influences the leader's behavior as well as those s/he is leading. Attitudes are infectious so that certain ones are more critical than others. Leadership is often stressful. Character is revealed during stress. Therefore, attitudes will naturally emerge if they are a part of a leader's character. Honoring others, confidence, servanthood, humility, and optimism are important attitudes for effective leading, especially during stressful times. The following are summaries and pump primers, ideas for adults to use in teaching good attitude skills that are depicted in the lower left quarter of the previous graph.

Quality: Honors People

Concept: People want to be on a team where they feel valued. *A good leader honors people.*

To honor is to choose to treat another person as valuable. Honor is the attitude a leader expresses toward others, regardless of behavior, personality, or personal preference. The four categories containing the sixteen qualities are flexible. Honor could easily fit in the relationship -skills quarter. The reason we've placed it in the character-attitude quadrant is because it begins as a way of thinking that results in action. Even when followers don't like a leader's decision, they will respect the leader if they feel honored. Honor is vital to effectively confronting performance issues, differences in opinion, and personality conflicts.

Pump Primers:
- Ask your young leader to handwrite thank-you notes to people who serve her, such as teachers, mail deliverers, refuse collectors, the principal, rabbi/priest/pastor, grocery store clerk, McDonald's manager, or coach. Leaders affirm team members.
- During a leadership project, make the primary task of the young leader to honor those involved with verbal affirmations. The goal is for the people to feel appreciated for being on the team.
- Do a melodrama consisting of a list of honoring and dishonoring statements. When you say something dishonoring or discouraging, everyone yells, "Boo!" Statements that are honoring and encouraging receive an enthusiastic, "Yeah!" For example, "You guys are lazy." "Booo." "Nice job, everyone. Keep it up!" "Yeah!"
- Leaders honor others by sticking up for them when teammates say or do things that are dishonoring. For

example, when someone insults or puts down a fellow teammate, even if joking, that person should be reminded by the leader that this isn't appropriate. Many kid movies and TV shows depict these situations. When you see one, push pause and talk about it. What would a good leader do in this situation?

Summary: While honor is similar to the concept of love, the latter tends to be thought of as an emotion. Feelings cannot be controlled. Honor, on the other hand, is a decision we can make. When you honor others, even competitors and arch rivals, you win the respect of those around you, a key ingredient for gaining adherents.

> **KidLead Idea:** _One of the biggest challenges leaders face in honoring people is how to confront unacceptable behavior or performance issues with an honoring attitude. The next time you need to confront your child, openly discuss with your young leader how to do this in a way that s/he feels honored. Let's say that you get after your child for failing to clean his room after you told him to do so. If the response to your correction doesn't go over well, make a note to talk about it later in the day. "Jeff, how did you feel when I got after you to clean your room?" Listen. "How could I say this in a way where you felt honored but I communicated my expectations as well?" Consider brainstorming some phrases that might help you the next time._

Quality: Exudes Confidence

Concept: Teams seek reassurance. _A good leader believes in the team and task._

Leaders exude a certain amount of confidence that translates into trust among potential followers. While this is often an unconscious, natural attitude that is telegraphed to others, there are ways to instill this quality. Experience is a good one. The more opportunities you can give your young leader to practice leading, taking charge, and being coached, the better. Sometimes confidence is little more than familiarity, feeling comfortable in roles of leading. That's the benefit of beginning early because most leaders don't begin gaining formal leadership experience until after college.

Pump Primers:

- Train your child how to meet adults. Teach him or her to offer a firm handshake, maintain eye contact, smile, and say his or her name clearly. Practice at home, and then extend this to others.
- Allow your child to pay the restaurant bill, find food items on a grocery run, and take on other tasks you'd normally do as a parent. This takes extra effort, but the opportunity to gain experience will increase your child's confidence as s/he becomes more familiar in these roles.
- Consider one project a week that your child supervises, whether it is overseeing a family responsibility or arranging a community service task involving peers. One of the reasons so many leaders are firstborns is because they have been raised in a world with adults and given responsibility with younger siblings.

Summary: Confidence is typically a combination of experience, ego strength, assertiveness, and personality. While some kids must learn to tone down their bossiness and overconfidence, most benefit from being encouraged. Reward demonstrated leadership behavior, and then assign larger opportunities.

> **KidLead Idea:** *Here's an activity that adult trainers use to improve the way leaders come across to people: videotaping. Record your young leader rehearsing to meet people and leading a small project. Then replay it so he can see how he's coming across to others. Provide ideas for improvement only after you've affirmed him generously. After all, we don't like this sort of critique either, even if it is beneficial.*

> Mike Huckabee, former governor of Arkansas and presidential candidate, tells KidLead about one of his early remembrances of a leadership opportunity.
>
> I saw leadership qualities in myself when I was very young. I was blessed by people who gave me wonderful opportunities early in my life. For example, I began a radio talk show for a radio station in our hometown as a teenager. I couldn't believe it, but the owner actually gave me the keys to the station. I'd go in and run the program. This gave me a lot of confidence as a communicator, which has helped me over the years as I became governor and then a candidate for the President of the United States.

Quality: Servant-like

Concept: People follow what is modeled. *A good leader is willing to serve.*

Humility and servanthood go together. Pride is a character weakness of leaders and is fueled by power and benefits, such as pay, privilege, and opportunities. "I'm better than you. You serve me," are attitudes that reduce a leader's influence. The primary role of a leader is to serve others by leading. Bossy, selfish, intolerant attitudes emanate from proud leaders. Therefore, a servant's attitude is an asset for leading well.

Pump Primers:
- Plan an activity with your young leader where you help a person anonymously, such as dropping off food to a family experiencing difficult times. Do it without anyone knowing about it.
- Brainstorm a list of "random" acts of kindness that you can do as family members. Tie these back to the idea of leading. Challenge your young leader to come up with a team project to help a needy person in your neighborhood.
- Community service projects are growing in popularity among schools, but most of these teach individual service. When

possible, try to organize your child's service projects in a group setting that teaches service in the context of leading others as a team.

Summary: We all want to follow leaders who are both confident and humble, but unless we as parents help kids learn humility while they're moldable, it's not likely to happen, at least not without a good amount of pain. Doing this early requires extra effort, going out of your way to line up acts of service, connecting with the needy, and setting aside resources to give. Modeling servanthood as a family is the best way to teach it.

> ***KidLead Idea:*** *Arrange a trip to help the needy. If you don't have contacts, ask a nearby faith community, or contact your local United Way office. Projects that can teach serving include working on a Habitat for Humanity house, planning a clothing drive for the area homeless shelter, or serving dinner to the indigent. If you have more possessions than the people you're serving, it shows young leaders how much they have and softens their heart to help others. If you don't have much, it empowers young leaders to realize there are others in need and that they can improve their lives.*

Jesse Nelson, on being in charge

When I was thirteen, I organized a project to take care of the lawn of a woman who cared for her adult, quadriplegic son. I called her and told her what we wanted to do. Then I asked my mom to drive my brother and me there with our equipment. I asked her to talk to the woman while my older brother and I did the landscaping. It was really fun being in charge and helping the woman and her son.

Quality: Optimistic

Concept: Hope motivates teams. *A good leader stays positive.*
Napoleon said, "Leaders are vendors of hope." Although times come when a leader must talk about problems, shortages, and pain,

ultimately the best ones are those who leave us with hope, because hope is a basic human desire. Shallow positivity that fails to consider potential risks and threats is not what we're talking about here; we mean rather tough-minded optimism, an ability to look at the giants in the land and still say, "We can take them." People nearly always select optimistic leaders over pessimistic ones. Therefore, emphasizing this in the life of a young leader is important.

Pump Primers:
- Create a pro-inventory list by writing down the good things in a young leader's life. When faced with a challenge, brainstorm positives that can come out of a tough situation. As you tuck your child into bed at night, share three "highs" of the day.
- Most things we fear never occur and are based on illogical assumptions. Create a worst-case scenario assessment of a situation that creates fear. This combines strategy with optimism by stating the worst thing likely to happen and how the young leader might respond to it if it were to happen. The unknown becomes known and, thus, less scary.
- Practice choosing words that are positive or neutral. For example, instead of saying "I don't like that food," suggest "I prefer other foods more." Instead of complaining, "We lost," say, "I think we've played better" or "We have more potential than we showed." A leader's words are important. Choosing positive ones makes a big difference to a team.
- Show how the inflection of a leader's voice can make such a difference in how people hear and respond emotionally. Have fun by making up a statement and then saying it in different ways, such as sad, happy, angry, bored, excited, and with intensity. Try saying, "This is a great day," with different inflections, or come up with your own.

Summary: Creating an optimistic outlook on life in general is fundamental to maintaining the same attitude as a leader. Melancholy leaders have a difficult time purveying positivity to others. The leader like a thermostat, setting the temperature of the team emotionally, based on his or her attitude. Rewarding optimistic outlooks is a great way to ensure hope in life and leadership on the part of a young influencer.

KidLead Idea: *On your way to school or a sporting event, take your young leader through a set of attitude exercises. These are called psycho-linguistics, or more commonly, mental calisthenics. Say things such as, "This is a great day!" "I feel good." "I am going to do my best." "I am going to succeed." Ask your child to repeat these sayings with you, three times each. Say them with enthusiasm and energy. This trains a child how to create positive emotional conditions. This is also a replicable skill when s/he leads teams.*

Research shows that parents can make or break their children. That is why developing a core foundation of what you want to teach your budding leaders is important. Jeff Nelson (our oldest son) did his college honors project on the parenting of evil leaders throughout history. His research reiterates the importance of why the positive parenting of influencers is so important to all of us. The good news is that there is incredible potential to influence young leaders positively so that they become constructive history makers.

In the final chapter, we'll introduce the KidLead training programs that focus on the materials presented in these last four chapters. There are over fifty hours of practical training in the four modules of **Lead***Now* and **Lead***Well* that is based on the content you just read.

Discussion Activators

1. What examples can you think of when leaders failed in the areas of these four competencies?

2. As you read the ideas on teaching these qualities, what other important leader qualities come to mind?

There are only two lasting things we give our kids. One is roots and the other is wings. This is especially true of leaders.

Chapter 16

KidLead Training Programs

Informed and Equipped

In the middle of writing this book, I got a call from my sons, who were stranded on the road. It was a Saturday afternoon. They'd left home late in the morning to drive back to college in San Diego after Christmas break. Just past Pismo Beach, Jeff's twelve-year-old Pontiac Sunfire's transmission wouldn't shift. They called AAA and towed it back to Pismo, where they got a hotel room to wait for me to drive from Monterey. I gave them our vehicle so they could get to school, leaving me with the lame car. The next morning, I was able to drive the ten miles north to San Luis Obispo, but then it quit again. I got a hotel that night until I could get it to a Pontiac service department first thing Monday morning. After a one hundred-dollar diagnosis, the bad news was that the car was going to cost more than it was worth. It wouldn't shift into second and fourth gears. As I was on the phone, arranging for a trailer to take the car home so we could sell it, the service manager walked by and said, "You know, you could drive the car home if you kept it in third gear." What? That's right. Third gear still worked, so sure enough, I drove it home. In fact, if we had that information before, Jeff could have driven the car to San Diego and avoided the towing, two hotel rooms, and a hundred-dollar diagnosis. But we lacked the information.

Information can change a lot of things. Most parents never seriously consider how they can develop the leadership potential of their children. They do their best encouraging school work and extracurricular activities, hoping someday, somehow, someone, somewhere will give them an opportunity to become a leader and unleash their influence. But now you have that information. You know how to begin to develop the leadership potential of your child and children around you.

I'm probably typical of many baby boomers who at midlife began searching for something more significant to do during the second half of their lives. I'm embarrassed to admit that my ego caused me to wait so long to launch KidLead because, well, I didn't think developing a leadership program for preteens was sophisticated enough. Although I value kids, I just didn't see myself working with them. But this really isn't about children or youth. It's about serious leadership, getting to leaders while they're still moldable. It's about impacting communities and governments and organizations for years to come by strategically growing great leaders. It's a matter of ROI (return on investment).

When people hear about KidLead, they want to know more. There is nothing like it right now, so their curiosity is piqued when they get an elevator speech on what it does and the vision behind it. Therefore, although sounding a bit like an infomercial, I'd like to focus this final chapter on introducing you to what has consumed my life over the last few years and what a growing number of people are becoming passionate about as they get involved with KidLead. The following leadership development content has everything to do with what motivated parents can do to further develop their children who exhibit leadership aptitude.

You've heard bits and pieces of it already, but by now, many are likely wondering how it works and perhaps even how you and/or your young leader might get involved.

Nina Lewis, KidLead Certified Trainer

One day after school there was a group of fourth and fifth graders in a room, hanging out before an after school program started. They were kind of rowdy because it was bad weather outside and everyone was tired of being indoors. There was some verbal pushing and shoving going on until one of the students spoke up and organized everyone with a game. He gave directions, told them it would be fun, and led the activity. The adults watching were amazed at the boy's ability to get control of the room. Just then I realized that this was one of the *LeadNow* students, who was leading everyone in one of the activities we'd done during training. It was impressive.

Training Curriculum

KidLead is a nonprofit, educational organization. Our passion is to provide world-class, executive quality training for preteens and teens. The active learning curriculum is based around the sixteen most sought after leader qualities, discussed in Chapters 12-15.

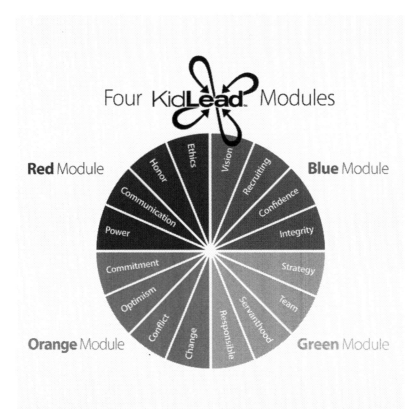

These sixteen leader qualities are divided into four training modules. Each module is color coded to avoid implying a sequence. Young leaders can begin with any color module. While all four combine to cover all sixteen qualities, each can stand alone. A typical module runs as after school or weeknight club meetings, lasting eight weeks in the middle of a semester. At this pace, a young leader would go through the entire program in two years. S/he could then repeat modules, coming back as a peer leader. These can be reformatted for camps, weekend retreats, and other venues, but a weekly rhythm aids in retention and application. Some schools are figuring out how to use them as class electives.

A typical club meeting is ninety minutes in length and involves two to four active learning experiences that teach one of the sixteen qualities. Activities vary so that a single meeting will include a combination of cognitive, micro, and macro-motor skills designed to keep the learner engaged. Youth take turns wearing a leader lanyard that designates them as the team leader of the activity so that everyone learns how to lead and follow. Each activity concludes with a debrief time for processing. There are various mini-lessons that last no more than five minutes. These are micro-lectures that explain a concept or provide an acrostic to give young leaders a more effective way of understanding the quality being taught. We also use kinesthetic learning through sign language and a symbol, to strengthen retention. There is a concept card for each of the sixteen qualities. Plus we recommend a media clip that ties in a popular preteen movie with a short leadership situation.

Teams are typically four to six kids in number, keeping the adult to student ratio very reasonable. The Certified Trainer typically functions as the emcee, introducing activities and overseeing the learning environment. A Koach is an adult or older teen who has been trained to facilitate team learning and who is supervised by the Trainer. A minimum size **Lead**Now or **Lead**Well club has ten participants, so there can be at least two teams, since some of the activities involve competing in order to simulate real-world pressure.

There is also a Leadership Challenge designed to be a fifteen- to twenty-minute at-home activity that reinforces the concept being taught and encourages the parent(s) to provide support. This challenge is reviewed at the following club meeting to emphasize responsibility and accountability.

KidLead places equal emphasis on methodology and content because both are needed for world-class quality learning. We designed the training programs with active learning, also known as experiential or accelerated learning, because it works best for preteen learners who are concrete thinkers. Experiential learning is also taught by the largest adult training organization, the American Society of Training and Development (www.astd.org). Even after a day of school and classroom teaching, participants are invigorated, and the hour and a half session flies.

Preteen and Teen Programs

Lead*Now* is KidLead's training program for ten- to thirteen-year olds. Our emphasis here is to target the 10/13 window, when leaders are still moldable in their character. The name reflects our belief that preteens don't have to wait until they are adults to lead. They can learn to lead now. Another benefit of focusing on preteens is that they tend to be less distracted by hormones and activities of older teen.

Lead*Well* is KidLead's training program for teenagers. While similar in nature, we realize that we have less chance to shape character, but we can still significantly improve skills. Plus, teens have more opportunities to demonstrate what they've learned and grow experientially by leading projects in their communities and organizations in which they're involved.

KidLead's strategy is to align with organizations that already serve preteens and teens. Therefore, we have a character-based curriculum for public, charter, and private schools and civic groups. We also have a faith-based format for churches and Christian schools, since these groups often work with preteens and consider it important for them to include scriptures and Bible stories in their training.

We encourage these organizations to offer *LeadNow* and *LeadWell* as part of their development programs. A certain amount of host branding is allowed to align them with their other programs. The host finds a qualified staff member or volunteer to apply and go through the one-day intensive training process. This qualifies the trainer to use the training materials as an independent agent. The training tuition includes the curriculum.

Costs

Parents apply for their child to be invited into the program. This involves filling out an application and completing two Social Influence Surveys on the candidate. These can be done online, at the KidLead website (www.kidlead.com). The Certified Trainers look for a certain level of observable aptitude so that peer learning can take place as young influencers interact with each other, their trainers, and the dynamic curriculum.

The Trainer or the sponsoring organization establishes the module training fee. These vary based on overhead costs, whether or not Trainers are able to donate their time, and what local scholarships may be available. KidLead recommends that these be priced similar to group music lessons or club level sports fees. Plus, research shows that people tend to value what they pay for, so we are opposed to giving training away. Even if local scholarships cover the costs, we strongly encourage Trainers to develop creative ways to include a monetary or bartering fee in order to increase the likelihood that participants will implement the skills they learned from KidLead.

A portion of the fee returns to KidLead to pay for the materials and to assist KidLead in operating as a nonprofit, educational organization. Trainers or organizations keep all additional revenues based on what they charge. This also allows trainers to earn part-time income and/or provide scholarships for more needy participants. Even though executive training programs charge $5,000-$10,000 for similar training, we understand the cultural perception that leading is for adults and lack of employer budget preclude charging such high fees. We believe we can prepare top-quality leaders at a fraction of the cost of these adult programs or university courses.

Each participant receives a shirt matching the module color, as well as notebook materials, concept symbols, and a completion certificate. Leaders become "members" of KidLead, receiving updates and ongoing training ideas. **Lead***Now* and **Lead***Well* grads are placed on a directory, designed to provide long-term benefit to them as they apply for jobs and universities. We believe this vetting process will create a reputation among organizations seeking to recruit effective, ethical leaders. We also hope that these grads will return to become KidLead trainers and Koaches, perpetuating a leadership legacy.

Long-term goals include a foundation that will provide scholarships for qualified but lower income trainers and participants, plus research projects. By remaining decentralized, we stay focused on the young leaders themselves.

Joel Osteen, bestselling author of Become a Better You and pastor of the largest church in the U.S. (Lakewood in Houston), tells KidLead about the value of investing time in young leaders.

I was so blessed to have a dad who really believed in us as children. He was constantly giving us opportunities to express ourselves and affirming our potential. I was fortunate enough to build on the foundation he laid. I think that's an important thing that a parent can do for a child.

I'm trying to do that with my own children. I don't think you can be a good parent unless you spend a good amount of time investing in them. That's why I have my office in our home. I get up early to do my work, but I want to be sure that I'm there for them for as many big events as possible, as well as a lot of little ones. It doesn't matter how much you achieve or how well intended you are. If you don't take the time to invest in your kids where they can see you modeling leadership, then what good is it?

Adult Training and Young Leader Research

Adults interested in becoming Certified Trainers should be leaders themselves and enjoy working with preteens and/or teens. An application process includes a background check, interview, references, review of a presentation video, and a full day of training that includes working with a group of youth. While Certified Trainers are independent, KidLead expects feedback forms and commitment to presenting the curriculum as designed to assure ongoing quality.

As we mentioned earlier, Koaches are trained and supervised by a Certified Trainer. These people facilitate discussion after activities and provide one-on-one feedback for participants leading a learning experience. There is also an application process for Koaches that includes background and reference checks and shorter training.

KidLead Trainers provide a complementary seminar called "Developing Your Child to Lead." This is applicable for parents and teachers working with children of all ages and includes a brief introduction to **Lead**Now and **Lead**Well. In addition to this workshop, there is a clinic for parents whose children are involved in the training programs, which covers some of the practical skills provided in this book for at-home support and training. As research suggests, a parent or guardian's involvement increases teaching retention and application.

As KidLead develops, we also want to provide consulting for organizations serving youth and become a catalyst for research. We want to better understand how children influence each other, we want to detect early aptitude, and we want to improve development during the formidable part of a leader's life. We encourage grad and doctoral students and other agencies to contact us for brainstorming ideas and/or sharing their results. KidLead advisory board members include respected experts in the areas of leadership and psychology.

Denise McBride, KidLead Certified Trainer

I don't think I ever "sensed" that I was a leader growing up, but I naturally assumed the roles. The earliest I remember taking a leadership role was at the age of seven. I attended a private school that year and met a music teacher who played guitar and led singing at a church. I began taking lessons from her. Before I knew it, I was playing for the church and leading songs. The class that I was a part of that year was very competitive. I remember competing with three other kids for academics and leadership roles.

Somewhere in my pre and early teen years, I lost my passion to lead. I rebelled. I think that is why I have such a passion to help kids and youth discover and develop their leadership talents. I want to help inspire them to stay the course of becoming great leaders. I believe that we can change our communities, nation, and the world if we invest in kids today.

Feedback

A training program is only as good as the participants say it is, so here's a sampling of some of the feedback typical of what we hear.

I like the challenges because they're fun and exciting, and everyone gets a chance to be a leader. –Nicholas (11)

We as parents have learned more about leadership, but perhaps the biggest benefit is Nicholas seeing himself in an entirely new light— an emerging leader. Along with greater self-confidence, he is building important life skills that will pay dividends. –Ed Powers, (Nicholas's dad)

*We've watched Karli's poise and confidence grow. It's fun when she comes home from school and explains things she sees at school in the context of what she's learned at **Lead**Now. That's also nice for us in a large family, where people are competing for attention in the chaos. KidLead has come along and nurtured her in areas where we see her gifts. Plus we have someone else helping us develop her and giving us direction.* –Katie Klinger, Karli's mom

*One thing I really liked about the **Lead**Now training is that you get to take turns being the leader in the different projects and activities. It makes it fun when you work with the team to try to accomplish things together.* –Jesse Nelson (13)

Channeling the energy of a strong-willed child by recognizing and developing leadership within these kids was a new concept that piqued my curiosity. But as a Trainer, the relevance of the program was confirmed as I watched, firsthand, young leaders blossom under the structure of the program. –Randy Henckel, parent and KidLead Certified Trainer

*My kids love **Lead**Now! They especially enjoyed the fun and relevant activities used to help them learn what qualities are needed to be a great leader; what a great investment in the future. The activities reinforced what they were learning and the Leadership Challenges were great.* –Margaret Morford, Cameron and Jocelyn's mom

Austin liked the activities, projects, and the interaction with others kids. It provided a step-up to do something significant, like his

project, which involved taking a group of his peers to talk to the principal about confronting a school bully. At eleven, I probably would have gotten into a fight. —Jim Pelichowski, Austin's dad

*The lessons brought up conversations that we might not have had otherwise. We talked about things such as leadership and influence. The experiences focused on topics we thought were good. We liked discussing the positives and negatives about leadership and were able to talk about kids in school who may be leading a group astray. We have Clay in scouts, chess club, and art classes, and you hear about it if he doesn't want to go. In every one of those, we've gotten pushback at one time. Clay never said anything negative about **Lead**Now. One night he was tired. We said, "It's **Lead**Now tonight." He said, "Great!"* —Ken Rayment, Clay's dad

Austin came out of the club meetings excited. He's not a big person to tell me details, but the kids were always excited about the leadership activities. I remember the lesson on integrity that helped me remember why that was important in leading. We remember the movie clips and found them helpful. We often talked about what they did in teams and we got to know other kids as leaders. —Julie Garrett, Austin's mom

*Paris never thought of herself as a leader. Since being in **Lead**Now, she now sees this ability in herself, and she talks about why she thinks she'd be a good leader because she's not judgmental and is active on the yearbook group at school.* —Mary Golden, Paris' mentor

Jack was very engaged, and I think the activities were well designed. They fit together very well. There was a very open atmosphere for creative ideas. A lot of leaders miss character in life. As I look at what's lacking in leadership in society, it's selflessness. I also really appreciated the parenting seminar and clinic. —Deron Grotelueschen, Jack's dad

*Kyle's enthusiasm around **Lead**Now was amazing. Rarely have I seen him embrace an activity this much, especially when he hardly knew anybody when he started. The Leadership Project Plan, leading to the actual project, was also a great learning experience.* —Shelly Scholtz, Kyle's mom

Vision

As of the writing of this book (2009), KidLead is in its early launch phase, after prototyping the curriculum the last few years. As with any learning organization, it will continue to evolve and improve.

Our vision is to identify and train hundreds of thousands of aspiring leaders around the world. To accomplish this vision, we'll need scores of people desiring to leave a legacy and invest in leaders who'll be greater than we were. This includes Certified Trainers, Koaches, organizational hosts, expert strategists, publicists, as well as corporate and private scholarship providers and financial contributors. The goal is for **Lead**Now and **Lead**Well to become communal, tribal tools designed to thwart incompetent and underhanded leading, replacing it with effective, ethical leading.

The business model is to operate from grants and foundations, large and small private contributors, and training fees and resource sales. This will allow us to provide subsidized, world-class training, but without undercutting the value by giving it away. KidLead is, therefore, in the market to partner with agencies and individuals who get what we're striving to accomplish and who understand the urgency and importance of this task. The residual effect will be more and better leaders in years to come, who will serve the demands of a growing complex world, which requires perpetual change.

Although we've provided a lot of information in this book, our underlying motivation for it was to cast a vision for rethinking how we go about leadership development. I challenge you to get involved. Perhaps it is by enrolling your child into a KidLead program or introducing a group of your peers to this book. Who knows what your divine role may be in influencing the life of a future world changer. We applaud whatever part that is.

In his book, *Outliers*, Malcolm Gladwell reports the inordinate percent of National Hockey League players born in January, February, and March. The reason is that in Canada, the eligibility cutoff for age-class hockey is January 1. That means that players turning ten in January have more than ten months of development on those born toward the end of the year. That's a significant difference so young. Coaches begin recruiting the better players for the best teams, resulting in superior coaching, more practice and between fifty to seventy-five games a year. By thirteen to fourteen years of age, this advanced experience and confidence are noticeable, and these top players are recruited for even more competitive teams and eventually the pros. Imagine what it would be like to give a ten to twenty year head start to young leaders. I'm convinced that we've yet to see some of the finest leaders in history.

I hope that you've been encouraged by the ideas in this book. I'm truly excited about the potential in a revolution that intentionally develops young leaders to be effective and ethical. We do have the power to significantly improve the future by influencing those who are and will be influential. I can think of no greater legacy than to leave the world in the hands of people like these. Remember, <u>if you want to change the world, focus on leaders. If you want to change leaders, focus on them when they're young.</u>

KidLead.com

If you'd like to communicate with Dr. Nelson for speaking, consulting, training, or media interviews, please contact him through the KidLead website. For more information, resources, and to sign up for a free monthly e-newsletter, go to www.kidlead.com.

If not now, when?

If not you, who?

-Hillel

Made in the USA
Charleston, SC
03 May 2011